MW01107033

FROM THE PANTHERS
TO THE PULPIT

Encountering His
Supernatural Kingdom

Library of Congress Cataloguing In-Publication Data

Scripture taken from the New King James Version®. Copyright © 1982 by
Thomas Nelson. Used by permission. All rights reserved. One New Man Bible:
Revealing Jewish Roots and Power, Copyright 2011 by True Potential Publishing,
Inc. Used by permission. All rights reserved worldwide. Scripture quotations
marked TPT are from The Passion Translation®. Copyright © 2017, 2018 by
Passion & Fire Ministries, Inc. Used by permission. All rights reserved.
ThePassionTranslation.com.

ISBN: 978-0-578-67851-1

DEDICATION

To the most wonderful, awe-inspiring woman I know, my beautiful wife Paula, to whom I owe my very life. Without you, I would not have made it through our first six or seven years together, let alone these past forty-eight years. Your grace and servant's heart truly reflect the kingdom of God and His heart. The world is definitely a better place because God created you and placed you in it!

TABLE OF CONTENTS

ACKNOWLEDGEMENTS

I want to give a special thank you to my son Joaquin Evans, our senior pastor who has been a constant source of inspiration and encouragement to me as we worked through this project; to the rest of my family, Paula, Jahi, and Kes who supported me and understood my struggles as I poured out some painful experiences onto these pages. Thank you, Eddie Tait, Maegan Tait, and Pam Spinosi, for constantly asking "When will that book be finished?" Also, to Naomi Specht and Allison Armerding who spent many hours editing this manuscript and Autumn Lorraine for her masterful and very creative graphic design work. I also owe a big thank you to my old friend Billy (X) Jenkins, the Black Panther Party Archivist, for his diligent research for this project.

And most of all I want to thank my daughter-in-love Renée Evans for her expertise, guidance and hard work throughout the entire publishing process.

ENDORSEMENTS

"The law of God is built into the hearts of men, and it will always reveal itself. In *From the Panthers to the Pulpit*, Jim Evans shares his own journey of how God's persistent love and transformative grace touched his life. From his life as a young man, angered by injustice and racism, to his survival in prison, to his decision to leave behind a drug habit for the sake of his young family, to his encounters with the God of miracles while exploring the occult, Jim's life testifies of the relentless pursuit of a good Father. Let his story stir you to compassion, increase your anticipation for God's intervention, and affirm once again God's absolute faithfulness."

—Bill Johnson
Bethel Church, Redding, CA
Author of *Born for Significance*, and *Hope in Any Crisis*

In his inspiring memoir, *From the Panthers to the Pulpit: Encountering His Supernatural Kingdom*, Jim Evans shares the transformational power of God amid personal pain and social injustice.

Within each page, Jim encourages readers with passion, freedom, and hope, revealing a beautiful illustration of the radical love and pursuit of the Father over us and the intentionality of his hand as he weaves together our legacy.

I highly recommend this book to anyone who, no matter the circumstances, needs a reminder that they can never escape the love of the Father—He is passionately in pursuit of you!"

—Kris Vallotton
Leader, Bethel Church, Redding, CA
Co-Founder of Bethel School of Supernatural Ministry
Author of thirteen books, including *The Supernatural Ways of Royalty*, *Heavy Rain* and *Spiritual Intelligence*

"In a time of such social unrest, anger & division, we all could use some hope and testimony of God's power to save!

`Jesus told us that we will know a tree by the fruit that it bears. Jim Evan's story is a journey from dark to light, fear to love and deception to revelation. When you know a man to be so completely surrendered to God and surrounded by a loving, godly family and then you read of where he started, you can only praise the Lord! For anyone looking for hope for a loved one or eyes to see what God is capable of doing in turbulent times, I highly recommend From the Panthers to the Pulpit to you! God bless!"

—Danny Silk
Author of *Keep Your Love On, Unpunishable* and *Culture of Honor*

"The life experiences of my friend Jim Evans display an extraordinary example of faith and hope along a journey marked by favor and friendship with God. A timely book with messages of transformation that are much needed today. Thanks Jim for sharing your heart."

— Robert Kinsella
Advisor, Strategist, Entrepreneur, and Minister

"After reading *From the Panthers to the Pulpit*, once again I realized the power of God's grace. It was grace that kept Jim when he thought his life was finished. Again and again we see the intervention of our loving Heavenly Father to help Jim and his family become burning and shining lights for the Lord. I recommend this book to all who desire transformation in their life."

—Jeff Collins
International Speaker and Evangelist

"This is an honest and vulnerable account of a man who has traveled a road that many of us reading this book do not understand. Thank you, Jim Evans, for leading the way in healing our nation by sharing your story.

We are encouraged to give ourselves to engage with our families, churches and communities in difficult conversation for the sake of unity and the Kingdom of God. We are inspired to dream big and to keep going no matter how far or hopeless our circumstances seem—knowing we have a Heavenly Father who loves us and has a "hope and a future" for us no matter the twists and turns we have taken along the way.

We can't wait to get this book into the Texas prison system to inspire and encourage the many men there who feel hopeless because of their history or even the color of their skin and trapped in a system over which they have no control—But God! We enthusiastically endorse this book and bless it on its way. May it accomplish the purposes God placed on Jim Evans' heart."

—Charlie and Judy Owens
The Joseph Company Prison Ministry
Huntsville, TX

AUTHOR'S NOTE

All accounts in *From The Panthers To The Pulpit* are true and accurate to the best of the author's recollection. All characters are real persons, but some names may have been altered.

FORWARD

The Civil Rights Movement had many heroes and polarizing figures. Whether their individual memories live on with reverence or are fuel for heated debate, their influence has affected how our society operates today and the fruit of their efforts will continue to live on. However, for every Martin Luther King Jr., Rosa Parks, and Malcolm X, there were hundreds and thousands of lesser-known individuals fighting for change and to see social injustice overturned. Whether fighting for change on a national level or simply trying to improve their own personal lives, they have all been a part of a collective momentum of positive change and their legacy, too, lives on.

This book is the life story of one of my personal heroes, and although his name won't garner the same recognition as the names listed above, his struggle was against the same social backdrop that fueled the actions and propelled the names of the aforementioned into our history books. As you read, you'll find the unfolding story of a man who refused to accept the status quo or yield to the social inequalities of his time. You'll be brought along as his journey to resist these inequalities evolves into a soul-searching, grassroots battle that plays out in a nearly unbelievable, but true story, that includes powerful, social, racial, and judicial reforms.

As meaningful as those reforms were, however, they never seemed to be enough and they never seemed to relieve the internal pain of the prejudice he felt or the anger he felt at all the social brokenness around him. His pursuit, however, did not end in vain but instead brought him to the end of himself where he discovered the only one who brings lasting restoration and reformation. The journey that began as a personal fight to escape oppression through battling external injustices ultimately and surprisingly culminated in an internal transformation through a dramatic encounter with Jesus

Christ himself, the Redeemer of all. He had finally discovered true freedom.

Yes, the hero of this story is my father. I believe, as you read these pages, you will be inspired as I have been inspired. His story may start as one of a radical revolutionary, who in his youth became embittered because of the world he faced every day, but it is also the story of a man who was ultimately transformed by grace. My father's story goes to show that there is no one too far removed from the grace of God that he is disqualified or discounted. My dad may have been a leader in the Black Panther Party but that was not the end of his story. He may have faced Nazi prison guards and led a hunger strike from inside Jail, which resulted in dramatic reforms, but that was not the end of his story. He may have been wanted and pursued by the FBI but that was not the end of his story. He may have also battled addiction for many years in his life, but that too was not the end of his story. His story is a testimony that anyone, regardless of where they are in life or how far they feel they have fallen, is only one touch away from being radically transformed from the inside out.

His journey reveals, what so many have discovered, that trying to battle the issues of this world by our own efforts will end in despair. But it also shows that when we reach the end of ourselves is when God can do his greatest work in our lives. We are called to be yielded vessels that God can mold in His love to be used for His purposes. But in order for the clay to be molded and shaped it must first be broken down and made pliable. In the same way, before God can mold us and use us, we have to become pliable and yield to His shaping. There are many ways God can do this but it is often the people who have endured the hardest lives and been subjected to the most tragic circumstances that God has prepared to be the most yielded and therefore be used the most profoundly.

You too have not been forgotten, and you are not too far gone, or too far removed that God can not use you in powerful ways. Regardless of whatever circumstances you find yourself facing at this moment or whatever hardships you've had to endure throughout your life, God has not disqualified you, and in fact, He has been preparing you for this very moment in time. My Father encountered Jesus while in a jail cell, facing a life sentence, and it transformed him, his future and as a result, his future family. If Jesus is willing to reach through the anger and rebellion of his life and touch him in a jail cell, then He is willing to touch you wherever you are, regardless of how angry, broken, or disqualified you feel.

Many lives were changed through my father's efforts as a revolutionary, many more, however, have been changed through the grace that now flows through his life as a transformed vessel in Jesus. As my dad's latter years have been in full surrender and dedication to the Lord, countless others have encountered the same grace and found purpose, love, and redemption. For many years now my dad has been in pastoral ministry. He has lived and served in three different cities and has operated in varying capacities of ministry over those years, however, regardless of our experience, education, or accolades, our most powerful resource will always be our testimony.

I know how my life has been impacted by the life story you are about to read, and I have witnessed its impact on many others. My prayer for you, as you read this book, is that you are the one who will be deeply impacted. Whether you have known God for many years or you are currently reading from a jail cell, I know God will use this story to inspire, challenge, and transform you. If you need God to touch you, read with an open heart, and I know He will!

—**Joaquin Evans**
Senior Leader, Bethel Austin

PROLOGUE

It was eerily quiet now. Blink, Al, and Phillip were all gone. Each man, having committed offenses deemed too serious to be tried by prison officials, had come to San Francisco to stand trial in Superior Court. Their cases now adjudicated, they had been returned to their "homes"—Blink and Al to Folsom Prison, and Phillip to San Quentin.

Like I said, it was eerie. I was used to constant noise and chatter. Now there were no voices. No laughter. No whispers amongst cellmates. The voices I was hearing I didn't care about. The crew who had stood with me against racist guards was gone. The men who had backed me on the hunger strike I started to protest the treatment of mentally ill inmates, and a dozen other causes, were gone. The guys I worked out with and trained with every day were gone. These guys had taught me how to survive jail and had given me confidence I could hold my own in prison.

The one benefit of this loss was that I now had a cell to myself. I also had a modicum of respect amongst the other inmates. Being accepted by Phillip, an accomplished martial artist, and Al and Blink, huge men known in prison lingo as "hogs," coupled with the fact that I had put on several pounds of muscle and had some martial arts background myself, helped quite a bit.

I could hear my friend, the prison librarian and trustee, pushing his cart down the cell block toward me. This man had recently saved my life when I was about to be attacked by racists in the shower. I owed him.

When he pulled his cart in front of my cell, he smiled and pointed to the two books he had left. Every day, by the time he got all the way down to D-block, most of the books on the cart were already taken by other inmates. He smiled because he knew I liked Louis L'Amour books about the Old West, and he had saved one for me I hadn't read.

As I reached through the bars for it, the other book lying there caught my eye. It was a book on meditation. The idea occurred to me that I could keep reading purely for entertainment, or I could start working on improving my mind, not just my body.

I grabbed the book on meditation. This decision would eventually alter the course of my life. It would be practicing meditation that slowly got me back into my old practice of praying. Next would come the shock and delight of my life. While praying, I would experience the voice of God's Holy Spirit!

THE BEGINNING

It was a sunny day in Greenville, South Carolina in the mid-1950s. I was five or six years old. I cannot remember the exact month, but the day I will never forget, nor will I ever forget the warmth of the sun on my face as we waited for the bus and the barbaric act that would soon follow, which almost took my young life.

My mother and I had come from Washington, DC to visit my grandmother and other family in Greenville for the summer. Though initially reluctant, my mother had agreed to let me accompany my older female cousin, Georgia, and her friend, both around fourteen and fifteen, on a shopping excursion downtown. Georgia and I were very close, and she assured my mother that she would watch and take care of me as if I were her own.

After the excursion, the young ladies, loaded down with shopping bags, and I boarded the bus that would eventually take us back to our part of town and to my grandmother's house.

Boarding the bus behind the girls, I plopped down in the open seat just behind the bus driver, where I was accustomed to riding on the buses in Washington, DC, my hometown. Unaware I had taken a front row seat, the young women proceeded to the back of the bus, as far back as they could get, as was expected of African Americans in those days in the South. This was before the brave actions of Rosa Parks in Montgomery City, Alabama, in 1955, so segregation on the buses in the Southern United States was still the de facto rule of the land.

As more people boarded the bus at that stop, I couldn't help but notice the glares from the white passengers seated in the front, and the look of utter disgust on the face of one female passenger in particular. She looked at me as if I was the most hideous thing a human being could possibly set their eyes upon. I turned from her gaze and found myself looking up into eyes of pure hatred. An elderly gentleman, who to my young eyes appeared to be a thousand years old, was holding a wooden cane with a tremendous wooden knob at its head in his gnarled, arthritic right hand. Raising the cane high above his head, the old man snarled, "*Niggerrrr*" in a low growl.

Time seemed to stand still. Having never experienced this level of evil from anyone, I didn't know what to do. I don't know if it was shock, incomprehension, or just plain fear that gripped me, but I sat as still and frozen as a statue. Then suddenly from my right I heard, "Don't you hurt that baby!" Georgia came flying out of nowhere, throwing her body over mine in an act of pure bravery and self-sacrifice.

The blow never landed. The old man was surely shocked into inaction by my cousin's instinctive yet courageous act. Refusing to look back at him, Georgia frantically pulled me to the back of the bus, where her friend sat in shock with her mouth wide open. While I will never know the man's reaction because I did not look back to see, I could not help but notice that the glaring passengers on the bus seemed to be angry with us instead of with the old man who had almost viciously split my head. I was too young to make sense of any of it. All I know is that the bus driver did nothing. The other passengers did nothing. It was as if this had been a very brief and insignificant event, and now that it was over everyone just returned to their own little cocoons, oblivious to the world around them. To the three of us, the hatred in the atmosphere was like a living thing, robbing us of our very breath.

My beloved Georgia had kept her word. She had protected me for my mother's sake and had faithfully and courageously acted as if I were her very own. As far as I know, my cousin never mentioned a word of the incident to anyone. While my world was forever altered, it was just another sunny day for the citizens of South Carolina.

CHAPTER 1

SHATTERED PROMISES

I was born and raised in Washington, DC. Growing up in Washington was a pretty rough place in those days, especially if you were black, and to be honest, still is. My Washington wasn't Georgetown or the Washington Mall. It wasn't pretty or scented by cherry blossoms in the spring. My Washington was crowded, rough, and seedy, full of violence, crime, and constant danger. It was one of several towns that burned when Dr. Martin Luther King, Jr. was assassinated in 1968. It was a city bursting with anger and frustration, a full pot on a hot stove just waiting to boil over.

Despite the tensions all around us, we kids always managed to have fun. We played ball on any patch of grass we could find during the warm months and slid down snow-covered hills in Rock Creek Park in winter.

Before we moved near Rock Creek Park in Northwest DC, the first nine years of my life were spent in the 21st projects in Northeast near Benning Road, and on Columbia Road near Georgia Avenue in another working-class section of Northwest. I regularly split time between my parents' apartment and my grandparents' house.

My first taste of street violence took place on 21st Street. I had wandered beyond the imaginary boundary line my mother had earmarked as the no-pass zone, which, I soon discovered, was set for my own protection. I meandered through the project section we lived in all the way down to the street. I was only three or four years old at the time, and there, in a patch of dirt next to the street, I found a little fellow about my age playing with some toys. He seemed to ignore me as I stood there. Neither one of us were very verbal as I recall, and I saw no reason why I shouldn't join him. Kneeling down, I started playing with a truck or some other toy of his. While I saw no issue with joining my new friend, he took exception to me. Just after I picked up one of his little toys, he reached over and punched me across the cheek! I was not only startled but also totally unprepared for a fight. Having no siblings my own age (my half-sister, Helen, was ten years older), I had no idea how to respond to any kind of violence.

Even though I was shocked by this sudden blast, I was even more stunned by the reaction of the adults who had witnessed it. If my mother had seen me punch another child over a toy, it would have been the end of me! Not only would I have gotten the whooping of my life, I would have been banned from playing outside for the rest of my life. However, these folks (some were clearly relatives as they called him by name) were applauding little Junior's aggressiveness, saying, "Good job! Look how strong he is! Way to go, Junior!" I still remember the laughter and pure zeal at seeing their little Junior impulsively use violence without a second thought. It was just another day in the neighborhood.

My second encounter with this type of aggression came about a year later. While playing outside my grandparent's home, a kid a year or two older than me, whom I had never seen before, came down the street, stopped, and struck me just outside my left eye. He then turned and walked back up the street without a second glance. To this day, I don't know if he was responding to a dare or if the devil made him do it, but it came completely out of nowhere.

Unlike the punch from the toddler, this time there was serious damage. The area around my eye was very swollen and bruised deeply. My family was furious and was certain the boy had hit me with something in his hand. My older cousin, Bobby, asked around and found out the boy lived in a tenement building up the street. As soon as I was able, my Aunt Lucille marched me from my grandparents' home up the street to confront him.

When we knocked on the door, a young woman answered. She was large for a woman and carried herself with the air of someone who was used to physically intimidating people. My aunt was a couple of inches taller but at least twenty to thirty pounds lighter. The woman looked at us with a mocking half-smile on her face, as if to say, "I know why you are here." After we explained exactly why we were there, she denied being the boy's mother, stating simply that his mother wasn't home. She may have been an aunt or an older sister, but she spoke with smug ease and authority.

Aunt Lucy was a very gentle, sweet, kind, godly woman. She was always positive, and I never heard her speak unkindly of anyone, even when others were engaging in negative gossip. But this day, my aunt was a force to be reckoned with. She stood her ground and demanded that something be done about the boy. As she was talking, the boy came to the door and settled behind the young woman's ample leg with the same mocking half-grin on his face. I remember a strong desire to wipe it off with my fist, and apparently Lucille did as well. She told this woman that if he were her child, she'd whoop him until he couldn't sit down! I could hardly believe what was coming out of my aunt's mouth, but the kicker was what came next.

"And if anything happens to my nephew like this again, I don't care if I know who did it or not! I'm coming back here, and I'm kicking some ass! *Do you understand me?*"

Although I didn't often hear cursing, I still knew it when I heard it. I don't know who was more shocked, the people on the receiving end of this tirade or me.

The lady understood, all right. Her only response was a mousy, "It won't!"

"You people ought to be ashamed!" With this parting shot, Lucille led me away. I never saw that young boy again.

These are the incidents in life you don't forget, no matter how long you live. That day I learned about family loyalty and unity. I also learned that in some families or groups, violence is encouraged, even though it was the opposite of what I was being raised to believe. It was so confusing, but just the same, my eyes were being opened to the world around me.

By the age of nine, my parents were finally able to buy a house, and we moved into a nicer neighborhood in Northwest Washington. It was in this "nicer" neighborhood that I witnessed one desperate soul stab another to death for a wine bottle on the corner of 17th and U Street. The next nine years of my life were spent trying to survive that "nicer" neighborhood.

In one aspect, I was luckier than most of the youngsters in my neighborhood because I had both of my parents. This was the exception more than the rule. For most of my friends, I didn't know where their fathers were; I just knew a single mom or grandparent was raising them.

Not only was it unique that I was raised by both of my parents but also that both worked hard! Though my dad had his questionable pursuits, he often had two jobs, one full-time and one part-time. My mom was a low-level supervisor at the US Treasury Department, and I'm sure she out-earned my father by quite a bit. She had some business college (as they called it in those days) that afforded her greater opportunities while my father had only a sixth-grade education. Though he was quite bright, the best he could do was a service position at the National Institute of Health, as well as various part-time positions as a janitor, exterminator, and other unskilled jobs that now I can't recall.

To this day, I am eternally grateful to both of them for the hard work and sacrifices they made for my sister, Helen, and me. My parents believed in education and constantly reminded me I could go far if I would only study hard, get into a good college, and graduate, something no one in my family had ever done. At the same time, they warned me never to trust a white person, and that no matter how hard I tried, I would always end up below the station of my white counterparts. Unfortunately, that was the way the world was as they saw it in the 1950s and '60s.

While this may have been the reality and belief of most, I wasn't having it. I knew if I was well prepared, nothing was unachievable. I was bright and willing and would not take "no" for an answer. After all, every TV show and movie I saw promoted America as the land of opportunity. It was a land of vast wealth and boundless horizons just waiting for ambitious young men and women to stake their claims and conquer its greatest promises!

27

My plan was simple: I would get into a good college that had an Air Force ROTC program, graduate, and become an Air Force officer and jet pilot. After a long and decorated career, I would become a pilot for one of America's major airlines, become rich, and retire happily with my wife and kids. It was a great plan, and despite the evidence and reality of the streets outside my home, I knew I could do it. I would escape this life where adolescent prostitutes, pimps, winos, and drug dealers inhabited the street corners. I would no longer see one man killed over a bottle of wine or young people carted off in handcuffs by the carload. My life would be different.

My mind was made up, and I worked hard to follow the plan. I was very active in my church, joining and becoming president of every youth-based club it had, and even became the most decorated scout in the history of my church's Boy Scout troop. I took ROTC courses in high school and joined the local chapter of the Civil Air Patrol. I was focused and ready to attack the American Dream with passion the moment I was given the opportunity.

While I was pursuing my dreams, the civil rights movement was in full swing. I paid attention to it but somehow felt removed from it. It was as if it was happening in an America in another dimension somewhere, like a Twilight Zone episode.

CHAPTER 2

LIFTING THE VEIL

I was watching TV one evening in my sophomore year in high school when I saw the unthinkable! Babies were being carried out of a bombed-out black church somewhere in the Deep South. The reporter's words turned into background noise as I sat there in shock and disbelief. I was stunned! My mind couldn't handle it, couldn't process what my eyes were seeing. All I could do was stare at the screen as these Sunday school babies were carted out of the ruins of their community church. Lifeless arms dangled from the sides of stretchers like over-sized rag dolls as loved ones screamed in grief and disbelief.

It was September of 1963, and the church was the 16th Street Baptist Church in Birmingham, Alabama. That day rocked my world, and I was never the same. That barbaric act is indelibly etched in my memory. It was as if the Twilight Zone suddenly became reality.

Soon after, a young black man in my community was shot and killed by a white, rookie DC cop. The young man had apparently snatched a woman's purse. This fact was not disputed, but what was in dispute was the young officer's account of the events leading up to the shooting. The officer stated the young man refused to respond to his commands to halt. Eyewitnesses reported the officer said nothing at all before pulling his weapon and shooting the youngster in the back of the head as he fled. Either way, the young perpetrator was unarmed. The African American community was up in arms, and after the authorities ruled it a justifiable shooting, the community's anger raged red hot amongst our youth, including me.

Things were further exasperated by another event soon after. Several white youths stole an expensive luxury car, went for a joyride, and led police on quite an adventurous chase through the suburbs and outskirts of DC until they were finally stopped and arrested. The story made the evening news. A few weeks later, these kids appeared before a white judge and were given probation!

People were outraged, but cries for justice seemed to fall on a society that was just plain deaf. The perception in our community was that justice for us was meted out in the streets. It seemed the court system found ways to forgive and rehabilitate white petty offenders while sending our youth off to imprisonment by the trainload. I was becoming angrier and more bitter, along with others like me across America, with each passing day. To us, the term "justice" translated to "just us" for white Americans.

When I reflect on that time in my young life, it is bizarre that out of the twelve or so young men in my circle of friends, only four made it out of our neighborhood without falling victim to prison, drugs, alcohol, death, or a life of crime. Three of us went on to college, and one joined the military. Thirty-three percent is not a great endorsement for achieving the American Dream.

The final straw for me involved my church, the place that had always been a haven for me. It was a place I counted on to provide stability, balance, standards above reproach, and some semblance of sanity in an insane world I just didn't understand. In church, I found men and women I could look up to, who provided guidance to help me maneuver through the chaos of life, in a world I felt was rapidly heading toward self-destruction.

The same year all of the events I've just recounted took place, the veil of naïveté slowly lifted from my eyes. I was about fifteen at the time. I had been so involved in church life and at church so frequently that I think the elders, pastors, and other leaders became somewhat oblivious to my presence and began to speak quite freely around me. I heard things I shouldn't have, things that led to further disillusionment. I heard about gambling activities, purchasing property they knew to be stolen, and other activities. I discovered that one pastor's daughter's mysterious disappearances were due to unwanted pregnancies and other things I will not elaborate on here. All of these things were common in my world but not in my church! The church was supposed to be a place of stability, safety, an escape from the chaos of reality, a sanctuary. My worldview had already been turned upside down, and the last thing I needed was to have the belief and trust I had put in my church fathers destroyed. I truly believed these men were practicing what they preached. Unfortunately, many of them, not all, were living duplicitous lives, teaching us one thing while practicing something quite different.

Looking back after decades of perspective, I have realized much of what I heard in church may have easily been explained if I had been mature enough to confront the people involved. Whether or not everything I heard was true or just the over-active imagination of a disillusioned boy, I now realize that human beings err, and these men were just men. They were subject to the same temptations and pitfalls of every other person in society. Though they should have been held to a higher standard, I had no right to judge them. But at that time in my life, these revelations shook me. The things I could count on to keep me focused on the promise of a bright future were becoming dimmer and harder to hold on to.

Slowly but surely the veil of my limited worldview was beginning to lift, the veil of the American Dream, and a just and fair world. I also began to see that my parents were mere humans as well. Later, I studied psychology and raised sons of my own, so I know that around this age children begin to see the shortcomings of their parents and realize Mom and Dad may have issues of their own. But I was already dealing with the fact that the world I had thought possible was not. I was beginning to understand people could hate other people vehemently because of something as petty as skin color, religion, or nationality. Not only could people hate one another— they could hate to such an extent they would murder innocent children in cold-blood while they were supposedly safe in church. I struggled with this reality for years, and I still find it unacceptable for any reason. I can only conclude that anyone who commits such an act is listening to the wrong god.

GETTING OUT

Something inside me changed after the day I saw the images from that church in Birmingham. A piece of me seemed to leave, and as it ebbed out, it was slowly replaced by something dark and malevolent.

While I never turned my back on Jesus, I became so disillusioned I soon turned my back on almost everything else. I wanted nothing more to do with church, scouting, or any of it. I went from a good student to a marginal one at best. Though I kept up a pretty good façade, I soon found myself not caring nearly as much about the things I used to, things like grades, honesty, integrity, and honor. I joined a "social club." While many called us a gang, we didn't think of ourselves in that way. Sure, we loved to fight, party, get high, and chase girls, but we were the best dressers in town and could out-dance anybody. We were the "fly" guys, the super-cool ones, and if we couldn't out-dance or out-dress you, we could no doubt out-fight you!

School became little more than a social outlet for me. If I had not been an athlete, I would have surely dropped out. Because I was pretty bright, I was able to attend school during the fall sports season, stay home most of the winter, and then return for track and field season in the spring. Most of my time was spent partying, getting drunk on cheap wine, and high on weed (most of the kids in my school had never even seen marijuana). With a full head of steam, I was charging towards disaster, and I would have completely self-destructed if not for a handful of people in my life. Two of them were my football coach, Coach Kauffman, and my seventh grade English teacher, Mr. Jones.

CHAPTER 3

I AM BECAUSE YOU WERE

In my junior and high school years, it became relatively rare for a competent white teacher or coach to stay in a predominantly black inner-city school. As soon as the community around the schools began to shift in racial balance, most whites, including teachers, fled to the suburbs. It was known in those days as "white flight." I'm sure the fleeing class felt it was a "survival thing," but for us, it was an "abandonment thing." This trend was just one more occurrence in the life of the average African American that sent the message, loud and clear, that we were damaged goods, unworthy of America's best effort. But we thought, Good riddance!

While most whites were running away from the inner city, a few decent souls decided we were worthwhile and, most of them made an indelible impression on many of us. The percentage of white teachers to black was probably little more than ten percent, making it fairly easy to recall them. I remember one particular man who had an impact on me: my seventh-grade English teacher, Mr. Jones.

Mr. Jones was young, bright, and energetic, and he gave us kids the impression that he truly liked us for who we were. He'd been an amateur boxer, and a pretty good one judging from the news articles he shared in class. We were fascinated. This "white dude" was trying to make us think he could fight! We thought it was funny, but knew he must have had heart to get into that square ring.

It wasn't long before our beloved teacher had the opportunity to prove his mettle. One afternoon, I had obtained a precious hall pass allowing me to go to the boy's bathroom, but if you were clever you could pretty much go wherever you wanted. I don't remember exactly what I was up to when the doors to the third floor of McFarland Junior High School suddenly burst open behind me and in came three of the most dangerous dudes to ever walk the streets of Washington, DC (and that's saying something). A young man by the name of Bernard led the group. Bernard-what, I never knew and didn't need to. Everyone knew who Bernard was!

Obviously, these guys were out of place. Being old enough to grow beards meant they definitely didn't belong in anyone's junior high school. The disruption brought our beloved Mr. Jones from his classroom to investigate. As he bravely approached these guys, who I personally knew were death on six legs, I could see him, in my mind's eye, going down in a broken heap. I knew for sure he was done for, and he'd realize how foolishly idealistic he had been to stick around when all of his white brethren had taken flight.

Words were exchanged, and Mr. Jones gave a stern command for the intruders to exit forthwith. Instead of leaving, Bernard, a huge and extremely muscular young man, took a swing. I saw my teacher's hands move smoothly and economically with no wasted effort. He ducked the first punch, came up, and delivered the sweetest combination of strikes I have ever seen.

Since then, I have spent many decades in the fighting arts and will share that part of my life with you very soon. But I've never seen anything quite as dramatic in real life as I saw that day! Before I could say a word, Mr. Jones had rendered all three unconscious. His hands were smooth and shockingly fast. He stood over the three, taking no joy or pride from what he'd done. I got the impression that, from years of practice and training, his reaction was automatic, without conscious thought. I was extremely proud of him, even though all of my comrades would have shamed me for being so—a white guy beating up three of the city's toughest! He became my secret hero, and I knew I wanted whatever it was he had.

I don't know what happened to Mr. Jones. Sometime later, I heard he married a very attractive young lady (he had shown us a picture of his gal) and took a teaching job in the suburbs somewhere. Wherever he went, I wished him the best, and I figured he deserved it.

The other white teacher who left a mark on my life was my football coach, Coach Kauffman. Coach had been the varsity football coach and athletic director at our high school for decades. Our athletic teams were highly successful in three sports—track and field, cross country, and football. Our other teams were highly competitive, but those were the big three upon which our athletic reputation was built.

I didn't try out for sports until my sophomore year, for a unique reason. Prior to my freshman year, ninth graders were still designated as junior high school students and attended the junior high school campus. My freshman class was the first to be assigned to a senior high school. The decision to move us came with little warning, and we felt like we had been given the greatest gift possible. We were now high school freshmen! The only problem was, technically, we were still designated as junior high school students. We were in the building but not classified as high schoolers! Consequently, no provision had been made for us to participate in high school sports or activities. It was if we were there, but not there at the same time. A few student clubs made room for us, but to most of the student body, we were intruders to be tolerated at best. For athletes, this situation was especially rough; we were in limbo. Our only alternative was to wait a year and try to make our athletic mark in three years, as opposed to the four the classes following us would have the opportunity to enjoy.

The fall of my sophomore year, I was encouraged to try out for cross country. I really wanted to play football, but was painfully thin for that sport. I made the cross-country team and excelled, finishing the season in the number-five spot on my team, which earned me varsity status and an athletic letter, something no other sophomore had ever done. I also placed high enough at the city championships to earn the city title for my team, beating out every other sophomore in the city and most juniors!

I was an angry young man, and my anger was the fuel I ran on. That year, I ran indoor track as well as spring track, and I soon became one of the best distance runners we had. Despite my success in running, I was determined to play football my junior year, so I showed up for spring football practice. Coach Kauffman took an interest in me right away. He saw quarterback potential in me, which made me about the happiest tenth grader in history. The only problem was that my track coach, Coach M, was furious. He had dreams of another city championship the following year, and I was a big part of those plans. The two coaches argued, but because Coach Kauffman was the athletic director, his word was final. He thought I should have the opportunity to explore any sport I wanted.

I was grateful for the support, but then things got weird. One of the assistant track coaches informed me that I should not show up for varsity letter presentation day, even though our pictures had already been taken and my lettermen jacket ordered. He said if I was going to play football the following year, Coach M was rescinding my varsity letter! However, if I changed my mind and ran again, I'd get my letter next year. In other words, I'd get the letter I earned this season next season, no matter how well I performed next year. I felt as though I'd been kicked by a mule! Given my recent experiences, this news was like throwing more fuel on an already red-hot fire. I don't remember my exact words, but I do know my response was neither kind nor respectful. I was furious and felt powerless and cheated by a world that just wasn't making sense!

It would be an understatement to say Coach M had a bit of an ego. He had a national reputation as a high school track coach, and he'd been written up in national magazines and local media. He was a god amongst coaches in our city. Coach M was a very fair-skinned African American who could have easily been mistaken as a Caucasian and was obviously a very bitter man. Many said he had been considered for a couple of very prestigious university positions until it became known he was not white. He loved to surround himself with white assistants, as I recall, and he had a very superior attitude toward his athletes. He was the most condescending to the darker kids and did not try to hide his disdain. True to his word, I did not receive my letter, though to this day it is recorded I lettered in cross-country that year (I was not nominated by him to letter in indoor track or spring track that year either).

But God was active in my life even then! While experiencing the unrighteousness of one man, He brought another into my life to restore a modicum of faith to my world.

Coach Kauffman was one of my heroes for more than one reason. One day, right after football practice, I was walking home smoking a cigarette when who of all people should pull up alongside me in his oversized old Cadillac but Coach Kauffman.

"Get in," he said, in his rough, gravelly football coach's voice.

I knew better than to disagree, and as I complied, I saw my football career dissolving before my very eyes. I was afraid I'd really blown it and was about to receive the royal boot from this no-nonsense field general, but instead of destroying all my football dreams, he talked to me like a father! He warned me about the dangers of cigarettes and how I could destroy a promising athletic career by adopting such a foolish habit. The hammer I feared never swung! I felt like a son being sternly but kindly instructed by his dad. His kindness was like an amazing, positive shock, and it gave me hope and a temporary balance point to which I could cling for a time. My belief that decent people existed in my world outside my family was renewed. While this act of kindness shifted my perspective on the world, it was another run-in that forever shaped my worldview regarding the races.

A RIGHTEOUS MAN

My parents were paying for me to have extensive dental work, including braces and several tooth extractions over a period of months, to straighten a severe overbite and correct a jaw too small for a normal set of teeth. Though insurance paid for most of it, I'm sure my parents went into quite a bit of debt to have this done for me. All this work had to be done after school, which meant missing a fair amount of practice during track season, but I was always careful to let my coaches know when there were appointments coming up.

One afternoon, I had a sneaking suspicion I had forgotten an after-school appointment. I had done this before, and our dentist was becoming understandably annoyed. He was threatening to charge my parents for missed appointments if I continued to "no-show," and I was concerned because I knew my parents couldn't afford any extra expense. With this in mind, I decided to call the dental office to see if my suspicions were correct.

There were two phone booths on campus—one outside the building and the other in a hallway between Coach Kauffman's office and the gym. Because it was convenient, in a booth, and therefore quieter, I decided to use the gym phone. When I got to the phone booth, I found it occupied by Coach Kauffman. I wondered why he wasn't using one of the two or three phones he had on his desk. It was very unusual to see him using a payphone.

I stood there patiently waiting for him to finish, but he stayed on the phone so long I began to get nervous about the time. Just when I was going to leave to use the other payphone, he emerged from the booth with a scowl on his face I'd never seen before. He was furious with me. I had seen him mad on the field before but never like this! He read me the riot act, giving me a very terse lesson on telephone booth privacy etiquette. When he had calmed some, I assured him truthfully that I could hear nothing through the walls of the booth and whatever his conversation had been about, the subject of it was completely safe! After demanding to know why I was there anyway instead of getting ready for track practice, I explained to him my dilemma. He seemed to accept my explanation as reasonable and calmly gave me permission to carry on. To this day, I still wonder what that phone conversation was about.

After calling my dentist, I found out I indeed had an appointment that day and had only a few minutes to get there without blowing it once again. My next task was to find a track coach and tell him I'd be missing practice. I prayed I would not run into Coach M, but I didn't have a minute to spare so couldn't be choosy to whom I broke the news. Of course, the first coach I saw was Coach M.

He was standing at the top of the main stairs leading down to the field in our bowl-shaped stadium. I called his name, and he stopped to face me. I tried to read his face, but his expression was completely neutral. As intimidated as I was by him, I plunged into my explanation as to why I couldn't practice, promising to bring a note from my dentist the following day. He looked at me with pure disgust and said, "Evans, you may lie to your mother and get away with it, but you sure as hell aren't going lie to me and get away with it! Don't bother to come back. I'm done with you!" He included a few other choice words in this exchange I have chosen to exclude here.

For a moment I stood there, stunned. There was a certain street etiquette precluding any mention of one's mother. It just wasn't done unless you were intent on provoking a fight! Later, I learned there are certain words that are legally considered "fighting words." Whether that's true or not, in the streets mentioning one's mother in any way, shape, or form is considered derogatory and are certainly fighting words. You just didn't do it, and I'm sure Coach M knew it!

My mind quit working, and all I could see was his throat. All I wanted to do was grab that light, cream-colored throat. The anger stemming from his prior actions and anger from every other damning and confusing thing I had experienced over the last twelve months or so swelled up in me until I lost conscious control of myself. Every injustice, wrong, hurt, and disappointment were all focused on his throat. I was a very thinly built young man, which earned me countless incidents of ridicule and bullying, but I was very strong (as all Evans men tended to be) and had been training in martial arts for a couple of years. I have no doubt Mr. M would have ended up at the bottom of those forty concrete stairs in a lifeless heap had I acted on my rage.

I was like a ballistic missile closing in on its target until I heard that gravelly and commanding voice yell out my name.

"Evans!"

Once was all it took. I froze, mid-stride toward my target. I learned that day the power of the "command voice." I have used it countless times in training thousands of martial artists over the years and have controlled many expert fighters with just a well-placed verbal command.

Coach Kauffman approached me from behind. In a daze, I saw him walk up to Coach M and insert himself between the two of us. Looking down upon M, with about six inches separating their noses, he told the track coach about our conversation at the phone booth validating my story. He also said he'd heard every word exchanged between us, warned Coach M he would be watching him, and if he ever heard him speak to another student in the way he heard him speak to me, he'd be looking for a new job. He also added that if Coach M valued his job, he'd better see me suited up for our next track meet, and as long as he was athletic director, he would not stand for such abuse. Now it was Coach M's turn to be stunned. He just stood there, turning crimson as a beet, knowing he had been caught red-handed by his boss. Having no defense for his actions and knowing he was not in a good position, he wisely chose to say nothing, but this little man was not through with me, not by a long shot.

Then, Coach K turned to me and told me to get on to my appointment. He never mentioned a word about what he saw me about to do. I will never forget that day, or him, as long as I live!

While I came out the victor in that incident, unfortunately my track coach got his revenge. Somehow the following school year, he became the school's athletic director in some rotation process the principal had instituted. I have no doubt Coach M had a hand in it, and Coach Kauffman was retiring and didn't fight the change. As you may have guessed, my old track coach had a surprise waiting just for me.

My junior year I played for the football team; however, I continued to act out in school and get into all types of petty trouble—fighting, insubordination in class, and the like. I spent a great deal of time in detention and in the office of Mr. Boyd, our high school principal. Mr. Boyd had also been my junior high principal, so we had a history, and not a very good one, and that history continued as he followed me to high school, first as the assistant principal and then as the head principal. Because of frequent minor, and some not-so-minor, disciplinary actions, my coaches had no choice but to bench me for most of the season.

My attitude left much to be desired, and I was having an increasingly difficult time responding properly to authority. I argued with teachers, missed a lot of class, and had developed such a bad reputation even innocent acts were interpreted as malevolent.

On one occasion, I was waiting for a friend to finish an after-school project in the cafeteria. Ronnie seemed to be dragging his feet, and I was getting restless. When he was finally done, I aggressively reached for my jacket, which was lying on top of a tall counter, not noticing that a pair of scissors, a heavy-duty tape machine, and several smaller items were lying on top of it. The tape machine landed on the foot of a female student with a loud thud while the scissors thankfully missed making contact with anyone. The young lady was very upset and accused me of doing the whole thing on purpose. I, of course, denied it, but she was insistent. I picked up the spilt items and placed them back on the counter as we continued to debate whether or not I was intentionally trying to kill her; I must have still had the scissors in my hand. She was furious and startled, though visibly uninjured and showing no sign of injury, fear, or weakness as she continued to scream and argue. I felt that same old monster called rage welling up in me and my control and reason slipping away. In a fit, I turned away from the students and flung the scissors at a far-off wall and kicked and shoved several chairs across the room. While I was not aiming these objects at anyone and no one was hurt, the potential had been there. It was a totally irresponsible thing for me to do.

The next day, I found myself in Mr. Boyd's office once again. This time we were joined by two rather large DC Police Department detectives, who informed me that I had been accused of assault with a deadly weapon. Evidently the young woman reported to the principal I attacked her with a pair of scissors and that I had thrown the scissors at her, along with several chairs. The principal wanted criminal charges filed.

I admit I was pretty nervous about the whole thing. I didn't feel I had done anything worth jail time, but you just never knew in these instances how things might turn out. I knew my fate was completely in the hands of others, and it was a very uncomfortable feeling.

The cops interviewed me in the principal's office with Mr. Boyd present. They also brought in the offended student, who was obviously scared to death! Her story kept changing every time she told it, continuously contradicting herself. The intimidating presence of the detectives, the principal, and myself in the same room proved too much for her, and I'm sure my glaring at her didn't help either. Fortunately, after interviewing those present at the event, the detectives concluded there was no case; the stories of the other students didn't align with my accuser's account.

I heard our principal speaking with the officers before they left his office, and he was pleading with them to arrest me, as he was sure I must be guilty of something. I was sitting in his outer office overhearing all this through the adjoining door, which was left slightly ajar. Was it on purpose? Was this just a scare tactic staged to give me a dose of reality, something to help me see the error of my ways? Could it even have been the tough-love actions of a tough ex-paratrooper trying to save a young man from himself. Unfortunately, I don't think so. A year later, this same high school principal would write on my high school transcript that I was not college material and was a young criminal destined to spend a lifetime in the penitentiary. That transcript would also be conveniently misplaced long enough after the admissions deadline to deny me entry into Virginia State University. Soon after the deadline, the university received the documents from my high school, and it was by speaking with an Admissions Officer by phone that I learned about these interesting entries. She stated she shouldn't have read these things to me, but she was astounded that someone would write something like that on a young person's permanent record.

No, I don't think Mr. Boyd was staging anything for my benefit. I think he truly believed I was a dangerous person walking the hallways of his school, and to be fair, he was correct. Though maybe not for the reasons he thought, I was dangerous just the same. I had a multi-headed monster inside me named anger, frustration, and fear, and was a very confused young man. I was carrying so much deep pain inside, and I had no clue how to deal with it!

Because of my many infractions causing me to not be able to play, I lost the quarterback position on the football team. With my very slight build, I was not well suited to play any other position, though I tried my best at every position I was given. Football may have been a bust, but thanks to Coach Kauffman's intervention with my track coach, I ran track that spring season and did extremely well. Our team was outstanding, and due to the hard work and dedication of the coaches and athletes, we were once again champions. Coach M was very pleased with the season's results and lavishly praised everyone connected with our effort—except me. I was excluded from every article, comment, and award ceremony. Following this, I became increasingly more sullen, angry, and rebellious.

In my junior year during spring football practice, Coach K once again designated me as starting quarterback. Though the responsibility of leading our very good team during my senior year terrified me, I was also extremely excited. I was determined to turn over a new leaf, and I couldn't wait for practice to start in mid-August, about a month before regular school began in September.

I only had one little problem. My parents didn't know I played football. From the very beginning, my mom was adamantly against me playing the sport due to my size. My father didn't agree, but as usual, wouldn't oppose her on the subject. I thought she was being totally unreasonable, and I wanted to play, so in a serious act of disobedience and rebellion, I had forged her signature on the parent's permission slip. Now a year later, and having the starting quarterback position back, it would be difficult to keep the secret. I had no doubt if I came clean, my dad would have no problem with it—in fact, he would probably be proud. But my mom would have a totally different stance all together. She would be furious! I decided to hold onto my secret until the perfect situation presented itself to tell them. As is usually the case when harboring a lie, this decision turned out to be a very bad one.

JW

I could count on my dad for support for most things, but when it came to opposing my mom, he just didn't like the strife. I loved them both dearly, but honestly where my mom was an open book and very predictable, my dad was a very complicated individual.

My dad was a sweet man. He was very quiet most of the time, and had a wonderful sense of humor. He had many friends because of his easy way and pleasant personality; however, everybody knew you didn't get JW mad at any cost! Once he crossed a certain line, there was no turning back.

The family loved to recount the time my father lost his temper toward another grade-school student. According to legend, my father had been relentlessly bullied and teased by this one student for most of their fifth-grade school year. Witnesses of the event, which happened in the one-room schoolhouse they attended in South Carolina, state that my dad had finally had enough. My dad was painfully thin as a young man, but that did not prevent him from grabbing the young bully, picking him up, and throwing him out of the classroom window. Fortunately, the school was house in a one-story building, so the young bully wasn't seriously hurt. He did decide, however, it was wiser to seek others to be the object of his bullying.

My parent's relationship was one of coexistence for the most part. Dad had long since given Mom full responsibility for managing the family, up to a point. She only had to leave him alone. They could talk, and she could ask his opinion, but she just couldn't interfere with his comings and goings or ask about his outside affairs, which, I think, were somewhat nefarious. My dad knew quite a few shady characters and was involved, I'm sure, in things that weren't always legal.

At twelve years old, I played in my first poker game with my dad in the basement of a house belonging to a bookmaker named Doc. Our host had his handgun lying close by on the table the whole time. I was often sent to Doc's house on "errands," and sometimes saw stacks of money covering the dining room table as well as stacked on side tables and in his china cabinet. Evidently, Doc was not worried about getting ripped off. I also ran "errands" for Doc, and he always paid me surprisingly well. When I was a senior in high school, I discovered that my dad kept his handgun in a bureau drawer in his bedroom. I knew my dad had guns locked away in the basement— hunting rifles, shotguns, and other kinds—but I was surprised to see that JW had his own piece for the streets.

One evening when I was a sophomore or junior in high school, my parents got into a very serious argument, and it got physical. I had been training in martial arts for some time by then and was pretty confident about my skills. I mistakenly thought I could handle just about anything. Responding to sounds of a struggle and screaming, I came up the stairs to see my father holding my mother by the hair. I could tell he was trying to exercise some control over himself but was not doing very well. He wasn't hitting her yet, but I could see by the empty glare in his eyes he was slipping into a state of fury where anything could happen.

I moved in, grabbed his wrist with both my hands, and was shocked to realize I could not move him. My father was not a huge man, standing at six feet tall and weighing about two hundred pounds, but he may as well have been a six-foot-five, two-hundred-and-fifty pound body builder! It was like he was made of steel, and as much as I tried, I could gain no leverage. I was having no effect at all, and my presence didn't make a bit of difference. I was seeing firsthand what many had spoken of in fear, and at that moment, I remember thinking how grateful I was for my father's policy of never laying hands on his children as we were growing up, in fear of his own lack of control when angry.

He was raging and only exercising a modicum of self-control. Fearful for my mother, I grabbed his right forearm with both hands and tried to pry him off of my mother, but I may as well have been trying to wrestle a steel beam loose from a construction site building frame. He looked at me with pure rage in his eyes and growled, "Get back, Jim!" I sensed this was a warning as much for my own good as it was so that he could have his way! However, I felt that the mere fact that he was communicating with me meant he had some awareness of what he was doing. I had never been afraid of my father, but at that moment I was very afraid. However, I was determined to hold on, whether my presence was having an effect or not. I felt I owed it to both of them. I wasn't sure how all this might turn out at all, and at one point the three of us almost went sprawling over the upstairs banister on to the stairwell. Then slowly, I felt the tension subsiding from his body, and his grip began to loosen ever so slightly. Eventually, he released his death grip on my mother's hair.

To my surprise, she continued to fight him. I thought for sure my mom had lost her marbles. Didn't she know how close she had come to complete annihilation? Now, my job was to calm her down before the whole thing started all over again. She finally turned and stormed into her bedroom, attempting to slam the door behind her. That door had been warped since I could remember and would never close all the way, but she tried her best. I realized how truly tough and fearless my little five-foot-three-inch mom really was. My father turned and silently went into his bedroom, and I melted down the stairs onto the first-floor landing, trying to stop my heart from busting through my chest.

Years later, I realized that pent-up frustration and a lifetime of dashed hopes and dreams were more the cause of their anger towards one another than anything else had been. My beloved parents were two bright individuals that life had played a cruel trick on. They were born in the wrong place and time with brown skin. Scripture teaches us that, "Hope deferred makes the heart grow sick," (Proverbs 13:12). This was never truer than in my household.

A year or so later, history repeated itself. The events were so similar that they almost blend into one memory. I had grown a little stronger, but neither my dad nor my mom was any weaker. Once again, I intervened to the best of my ability. The results were almost identical, except that this time, my dad left the house. This seemed to be a ritual they were doomed to repeat. I have no idea how they managed after I left home. I have no doubt they had deep affection for one another, but once respect has been lost, I don't think love can survive. I think they simply mellowed with age and decided to enjoy the time they had left. I never got a sniff of any further conflict between them, and I hope there was none.

CHAPTER 4

IT BIT ME

Going into my senior year, I was very excited. I would be a senior and the starting quarterback on our football team, and was determined to work hard, both physically and academically.

That summer, we took our traditional trip to South Carolina to visit relatives. Both my parents were raised in the same area, though they didn't meet until they were adults living in New York City. My father was fresh out of the army after serving in the Pacific during World War II, and they were introduced by mutual friends and started dating soon after. Most of his relatives had migrated north, seeking jobs during the Great Depression years, but many of my mother's family had remained in South Carolina, including my grandparents and several of her brothers and sisters. She came from a family of seven siblings.

After a few days of visiting, we decided I would stay in South Carolina with family while my parents traveled a bit and returned to work in DC. I didn't mind this, but reminded them, without saying why, that I had to be back home no later than mid-August.

The summer drifted by. I enjoyed hanging out with favorite cousins and their friends, playing sports, and pursuing summer romances. I didn't get to speak to my parents very often. They didn't seem to be home much and there was no way to leave messages at our home, as this was before answering machines. When I was able to reach them, I never ended our conversation without reiterating our understanding about when they would come for me. I wanted to make sure they understood. Within a week or so of the agreed-upon date, however, they seemed to have disappeared, and I couldn't reach them anywhere. I called our home every day and even left messages with aunts and family who lived nearby. Nothing! The appointed day came and went. Nothing! I called. Nothing. I left messages with friends and relatives. Still nothing.

Seething with anger and disappointment, I resigned myself to the fact that they weren't coming until the last minute, that they really hadn't heard me but were placating me with convenient answers and promises to come for me earlier. I was reminded of the old saying that "children were to be seen and not heard." This little colloquialism can denote proper behavior for a child in adult company—that they should not interrupt, stand politely until spoken to, or blend into the background and not have an assertive presence. But it can also mean that the wishes and demands of a child, outside his basic welfare, are secondary to the wishes and desires of adults. In much of American culture today, children's slightest desires are a major priority to the parents. In some instances, the children hold a loftier position of priority in the family than the parents. In pre-1970s black culture, however, this was definitely not the case. Children were not to be spoiled at any cost. You didn't owe them an explanation for any action you took, even if it meant breaking a promise.

When my parents came, they had no explanation for the delay. As a matter of fact, their only response was a blank look, as if to say,

"What are you talking about?" I finally made it home just in time for the first day of school. The team had been practicing twice a day for about three weeks by then, and the starting quarterback position had been given to my friend and martial arts partner, Richard. Richard was very good, we had an okay season, and though disappointed, I supported him wholeheartedly.

After several weeks of loathing, it did eventually occur to me who the real villain was in all this. I was the dishonest one. If I had been honest and forthright from the beginning, I might have taken some heat for deceiving them, but it would have been over. I knew my parents—if I had confessed earlier and asked for and received their forgiveness, they would have gotten me back on time or would have forbidden me to play. Either way, it would have been settled, and all this discord would have been avoided. The blame rested squarely with me, and I eventually accepted that fact. I had to take responsibility for my own actions. I could not continue to blame others for outcomes resulting from the choices I made. It was a valuable life lesson, and one I never forgot, for that lie had come back to bite me in the rear.

Before closing this chapter of my life, I have to finish telling you about Coach M, the man who had it out for me. Since football and cross-country seasons took place at the same time, I could not participate in both. By my senior year in high school, I had not run cross-country for two years but had run spring track and done very well. There was even talk of a scholarship to Virginia State University. Because of my success in the sport, I was very excited as spring track season approached in 1966, my senior year.

A day or two before the first day of practice, I excitedly went down to the equipment room to get my practice and meet uniforms and gear. When I arrived, the equipment manager told me there was nothing there for me. Coach M was only inviting select athletes to participate in track this season, and I wasn't on the list. I told him there had to be a mistake since I was the best distance runner the school had. He checked the list again. I wasn't there. He eventually confided that Coach M told him the absence of my name was no mistake. He had been instructed that under no circumstances was I to be given any equipment.

Though I was puzzled, a sinking feeling of certainty began to form in the pit of my stomach. Could he be that vindictive? He knew I had a scholarship pending. Would he go that far?

I went to his office, but he wouldn't see me, so I went to Coach Kauffman. While he sympathized with me, there was nothing he could do since he was no longer the athletic director. I went back to Coach M, but he still wouldn't see me.

I was devastated. It seemed every time I tried to turn my life around, I was shot down. It left me wondering what I was supposed to do: sulk, fight, cause a disruption? What? I had taken responsibility for all my prior screw-ups, and now this. I really wanted to hurt somebody, so I did—I hurt myself. Once again, I stayed away from school for weeks.

I stayed home during the day, watching TV and eating. I pretended to do homework at night but just read comics. I came to a few track practices to see if the almighty coach would change his mind, but he only turned his back to me, refusing to exchange even one word with me. His silent communication came through loud and clear: "You think you got away with something hiding behind your football coach, but I have the last word. Who's screwed now?"

I did have one last bit of satisfaction, however. Coach M had told my teammates I had chosen not to run that year. He told them I was too lazy and didn't care about the team or our chances that season, which, of course, puzzled them all. They knew about my scholarship possibilities, since anything to do with plans of playing at the collegiate level is a major source of conversation amongst most high school athletes. Those I was close with knew I wanted to run and was looking forward to the season. So, of course, my team wanted to know why I wasn't suited up and on the track. Our equipment manager, under penalty of exile, had told a couple of the guys what coach had done, but most were in the dark. Once I related the truth to my team, they were furious. Some confronted the coach, and over the next two to three weeks, some members quit the team, including a couple of our younger distance runners, sprinters, and hurdlers as well (some jeopardizing their own scholarships). I was shocked and extremely grateful for the solidarity my friends had shown, which was pretty much unheard of.

That year, for the first time in recent history, our school did not finish in the top three in the region. If memory serves, we finished somewhere around fifteenth. Coach M got his revenge, but he did not get his championship.

During this season of my life, I learned a couple things: 1) lying may get you short-term gain but leads to bitter disappointment and loss, and 2) evil men exist, but there are plenty of righteous ones as well.

CHAPTER 5

THE MARTIAL WAY:
GRAND MASTER KI-WHANG KIM

During my ninth-grade year, I began studying martial arts. A friend told me about a Korean man teaching a free class in something called taekwondo. I had never heard of it, but it was supposed to be hard, tough, focused on punching and kicking, and requiring sharp focus and discipline. Considering all of this, it sounded like it was made for me.

I'd given judo a try for a few weeks but was terrible at it. As I've already stated, I was tall and skinny and had no muscle to speak of. I wasn't a weak kid, but I just had "nothing in the wallet," as the saying goes. One of the school football coaches was the judo instructor; he was a terrible coach and even worse teacher. He continually paired me with the biggest muscle-bound guy in the class. I could do nothing with him and often found myself plastered against one padded wall after another. What made matters worse was the teacher was completely unaware of what was going on during class. After he demonstrated what he wanted you to perform, he seemed to disappear. He might as well have been on the moon as far as I was concerned, since he was never available to explain anything or instruct my over-sized partner to slow down a bit before I broke. I soon quit, having learned nothing but how to stack bruise upon bruise.

Unlike judo, this taekwondo sounded perfect. I was good with my hands and could "throw" with the best of them. The only problem was, once my guard was penetrated and things broke down to a wrestling match, I was at a huge disadvantage and usually got my butt kicked. Thankfully, I was good enough that this rarely happened. During late elementary school and early junior high (fourth through seventh grades), I averaged a fight per week. That is no exaggeration. Some of this had to do with my build making me appear to be easy prey, but most of it was due to our environment and my attitude. Our neighborhood was violent, and if you ran with the thugs (or even if you didn't to some degree) you couldn't escape the violence. Truthfully, I never fully understood the rationale behind all the fighting and I hated fighting anyone I considered a friend, it was just part of the scenery, a ritualized lifestyle. It came with the territory.

With all this in mind, the class sounded great, and I decided to check it out. That single choice turned out to be one of the best decisions I have ever made.

I went to a class at the YMCA on 11th Street in Northwest Washington, DC, and met Master Ki-Whang Kim. He was of average height for a Korean and was very strongly built. I was blown away by what I saw. This instructor seemed to know exactly what was going on in his class at all times, and though he spoke no English, none, he was more than capable of communicating exactly what he wanted done on all levels. He paid great attention to detail and had students repeat the smallest movement until it was done perfectly, while smiling almost continuously. Although he appeared to be friendly and completely relaxed, the students responded to his every gesture with instant obedience, so you could tell he was not a man to be trifled with.

I joined his class and enjoyed every minute of it. Class was twice per week and most days I walked the twelve blocks there, preferring to keep the bus money I had for other purposes. This class was the most demanding activity I had ever been involved in. Master Kim was a taskmaster, and he would often keep us in a deep horseback-riding stance, juchoom suhgi, with our knees bent for thirty minutes, which felt like hours after walking twelve blocks just to get there. He would then take us to another short activity and then right back to another deep stance while we traded punishing forearm blocks, pahkat hulio mahki, or reverse punches, bahndae chigi, against one another until our arms and bodies were bruised to deep purple and had lost all feeling. Then, of course, I had to walk another twelve blocks back home.

In those days, early-to-mid-1960s, we had no safety gear or padding, so I was often sore and bruised for days after class. Master Kim only had us twice a week for a couple of hours, so he was determined to make the most of it. As I mentioned earlier, this man spoke no English, but he did speak perfect bamboo stick. We all soon learned the meaning of a sudden and painful slash across your arm or leg with the bamboo stick. It was very basic yet effective communication. You either understood or quickly (and secretly) asked someone else. There were no excuses or debating. It was perfect behavior modification—you didn't want the stick, but you did want the smile. The training was "old school" and hard, except for the short hours. I'm sure Master Kim taught us using the same training methods he experienced as a student in Korea, minus the eight-hour training days many Korean kids endured in the rural villages.

I was fortunate, in this regard, to have a string of master instructors (many of whom went on to become revered grandmasters) who taught by the old ways. I was a member of one school where the training was so intense, I came home with blood on my uniform every night. Modern training is now so politically correct that it has become soft. I don't advocate abuse by any stretch of the imagination, but I do advocate tough and proper preparation. My instructors were not inhumane or cruel by any means. They were not Karate Kid movie villains, but they did prepare us to deal with any adversary under any circumstance in a real-world setting, which, quite honestly, kept me alive more than once.

Master Kim was one of several Korean instructors to come to the US in the late 1950s and early 1960s. I can't name them all, but some of the notables were Richard Chun of New York City, Daeshik Kim of the University of Texas-Austin, and Ken Min of UC Berkeley. The man most readily recognizable by the American public, and known as the instructor to Capitol Hill, is probably Jhoon Rhee, also of the University of Texas and later Washington, DC, where he made his home in the early 1960s.

The men I've written about in these chapters were my saviors. Without the positive influences of men like Mr. Jones, Coach Kaufman, and Master Kim, my life would have turned out very differently. The choices I've made since that era in my life have not all been perfect by any means, but I know I would not have had the character, courage, and fortitude to walk the path I have without the good fortune to receive from their teaching and example.

By crediting these men with being my saviors, I don't mean to diminish the positive support and influence I received from my family. My parents, as all do, had their problems, but they were also there for me when I needed them and were great providers. We lacked for no necessity. I was very confused and not very honest with them during my teen years, which, of course, prevented them from helping as much as they could have. My grandparents on both sides were wonderful, and I received unconditional love from the four of them. I also was close with my sister, several aunts, uncles, and cousins.

But these men gave me a critical rebuttal to racism. Our society was very racially closed during this era and for years to come. However, these men reached across racial boundaries when others wouldn't. I learned lessons more valuable than gold from these teachers, lessons contradicted by generations of beliefs and conditioning. I learned lessons not easily obtained or received by my peers, that you take each man and woman for who they are as individuals, you seek the gold in each person, and if a person is willing to share, there is usually something worth learning from them.

Countless times since, others have judged me strictly by appearance. Years later, when I was CEO of a home healthcare company my wife, two partners, and I founded in Ojai, California—a predominately white, upper-middle-class town of artists and Hollywood professionals—a young salesman walked into my inner office to find me sitting behind my desk. My secretary/marketing coordinator was on a marketing visit, our operational offices were on another floor, and our two administrative offices were set apart from the rest of the company's operations, making it possible for him to walk right in without interference. Upon seeing me, he seemed instantly confused. I was sitting there in a three-piece suit, working at my desk with a nameplate clearly visible. He did a double take, looked around in confusion, and asked me when Mr. Evans would be back at his desk. I looked up, smiled and said, "You are talking to him. How can I help you?" I wish I'd had my office rigged with hidden cameras. It was one of the most hilarious things I'd ever seen. The young man turned several shades darker (any darker and I would have been tempted to call him "brother"), looked around vainly for some place to hide and wait for help that was not forthcoming, and finally decided to just plunge forward with his sales pitch. As he stumbled through with embarrassment clearly evident on his face, I was reminded of the lesson I had learned three decades earlier—don't judge before you know.

This type of almost comical interaction is not unique to me alone. We all profile to a certain extent. It's a survival mechanism we use to assess if someone or something is a potential threat or friend. But when race, speech, or appearance is the only measuring stick used, one runs the risk of excluding "angels" from one's life.

CHAPTER 6

RADICAL ANGER

As you know, I was a very angry young man. To be honest, I don't believe I was angrier than most other young black men in my community—perhaps angrier than some but probably less than others. The one thing I am sure we all had in common was confusion. Most of us were angry, and some consumed in hate, but if you had picked any of us out at random and asked why we were so angry, you would have received no real answers, just a ball of emotional sputum. You would get answers like, "I'm angry at The Man, or The System," or "Because They are against us," but I doubt any one of us could have articulated the real reason for our anger, and even hatred, at that age.

The majority of us were too young and sorely lacking any real tools for cultural self-analysis. If we had been equipped to deal with such a question, we would have told you the cause of all our anger, hate, and confusion was due to one thing—the death of dreams!

"Hope deferred makes the heart sick, but when the desire comes, it is a tree of life." (Proverbs 13:12)

It is a hard thing to awaken one day and realize your dreams have died and you have no future, or to realize there is an invisible ceiling above your head not only blocking you from reaching your dreams but actively attempting to extinguish you. Some essence of life escapes from your very soul when you realize the sky is no longer the limit, but in fact the whole premise of unlimited opportunity was just a very cruel lie.

Trust me, I'm not attempting to make excuses here. I'm not in need of a crutch or a reason why I failed to accomplish this or that; I'm simply explaining the mentality of a generation. Take away hope, and you are left with doom.

I know many in American society have had to struggle, claw, and fight for a piece of the American Promise. If you were a person of color in that time in American history, it was not a matter of changing your last name, escaping a neighborhood or an abusive or negligent parent, or renouncing your religion. Your skin followed you wherever you went, and to us, it seemed we could not go far enough to escape the nightmare we had awakened to. The powers-that-be were willing to kill us and our heroes who were willing to stand up for justice and represent a disenfranchised people: Medgar Evers, John Kennedy, Robert Kennedy, Malcolm X, Martin Luther King, Jr.…you name them.

In my case, because of my family's beliefs (though admittedly the signals from them were mixed) that I could accomplish great things, and because of the influences of coaches, teachers, and instructors in my life, I refused to allow my dreams to completely die.

As time went on, in order to cope with their reality and the continuous crushing of their hopes and dreams, many of my friends turned to alcohol, drugs, or crime. The drugs and alcohol numbed your mind and dulled the pain. When high, you no longer had to think or feel, and when you became a criminal, an outcast from society, you were thumbing your nose up at The Man. You were making the statement you could do just fine without his rules and accepting his conditions. You could do very well indeed, doing it your way.

As for me, I decided to fight! But how?

CHAPTER 7

MAKING A CHOICE

After barely graduating high school, I decided to take a new approach. The choices were clear: become a very inept criminal (hard as I tried at times, I just didn't seem to have the aptitude), dive into drugs and/or alcohol, scratch out a meager living at a menial job the rest of my life, or go to college. College seemed like less work and definitely had a brighter upside, so I enrolled the next fall in Montgomery County Junior College.

I spent one semester at the junior college and rediscovered the student in me. If I remember correctly, I only took two classes, one being English, and got two As. I surprised myself, and this success rekindled something in me. I suddenly had a new academic confidence.

My next stop was Western Nebraska. Due to poor grades in high school and my principles lovely note in my transcript, I didn't exactly have colleges beating down my door, so my choices were fairly limited. Friends of my parents told them about this wonderful school their son was attending; they raved about it. We met with a recruiter who promoted it as the Yale of the Midwest, so I applied and was accepted. This inner-city, East Coast kid took off for Western Nebraska.

It turned out to be a big lie. There was a college there in Scotts Bluff, Nebraska all right—that much was true. It consisted of one administrative/classroom building, one completed dorm, and two motels doubling as dorms, which filled with sand with the slightest wind. I attended Hiram Scott College for two years. I even made the dean's list the first semester—but then racism raised its ugly head.

One day, soon after arriving in Scotts Bluff, I was standing on a street corner waiting for a red to turn green when a Native American gentleman came up beside me. I had never seen a Native American (that I knew of) in person before. I may have stared, I honestly don't know. Anyway, I said hello to him, and his response stunned me. He looked over at me with disgust, a look I'd seen many times before, spat down at my feet (missing me by inches), and walked away. Like I said, I was stunned—too stunned to move. I stood there until the light turned red again. I learned later that there was a racial pecking order in the region—whites first, Hispanics second, Native Americans third, and blacks last. Welcome to the Deep South, I mean the Midwest.

Making the dean's list proved to be more difficult than it should have been. I made the 3.0-plus GPA, but it should have been higher. I took a music class the following two semesters that I loved. The instructor was a real music lover and introduced us to traditional and modern classics. It opened me to more than just rhythm and blues, jazz, and the blues, like Dave Brubeck's work. I carried a B average the first semester and an A average the second, but when it came time for my final grade, I received Ds both times. When I confronted the professor, I was informed, after several unsuccessful attempts at trying to lay blame on my attendance (which was 90%), that a black student would never receive better than a D from him, no matter his or her achievements.

This was another insult in a long line of insults. I was angry and complained to the dean, but was told there was nothing he could do. Once again, I found myself in a situation where I had no recourse. I had had enough.

As blacks, we were egged or spat upon every time we went to town a few miles away from campus. We were attacked and frequently had to defend ourselves from the violence of local townsmen. One night, someone stood outside the ground-floor window of my best friend's dorm room and unloaded a shotgun into it, shattering the glass and striking his bed. His bed, where he should have been sleeping, was riddled with shotgun pellets. I personally saw the scene just after the shooting, and there is no doubt in my mind Gerry would have been dead if he had been in his bed. The shooter or shooters were definitely aiming for his bottom rack, exactly where they expected him to be.

It was obvious the incident was racially motivated. When we got to his room, a huge burning cross could clearly be seen through his dorm room window just a few feet away. Gerry had been seeing a white girl from town for several weeks and dealt with death threats every time he went to town. Young men would scream, "We're gonna kill you, nigger!" outside their car windows as they drove by. The young woman had been ordered by her father to stop seeing him and was being harassed in town as well. Fortunately, a few of us insisted he join us in a card game that night on a different floor of the dorm. We were actually acting like jerks as we drug him, practically in his underwear, to the game upstairs. We didn't realize, at the time, we were saving our friend's life.

As far as we knew, nothing was ever done—no investigation, nothing. The college maintenance crew did repair the window, however. Gerry and his girl eloped. He took her back home with him to Pennsylvania.

You might say this was a bad experience, a part of my life I'd just as soon forget. Even so, two things happened for me in Scotts Bluff, Nebraska. I made a life-long friend, André Russell, and I decided to start fighting back.

THE BLACK PANTHERS ARRIVE

In the winter of 1967, several black students and myself started a Black Student Union (BSU). Our agenda was simple: band together, educate one another, and defend ourselves from violent attacks. The BSU also gave us a voice to present our grievances to the administration, and it seemed to work very well.

The pivotal point for me was the day we received a communication from the newly formed Black Panther Party (BPP). Though the BPP was formed in Oakland in 1966, it grew rapidly across the nation. By 1967, there was a chapter established in Denver, Colorado. The Denver chapter had heard about us and wanted permission to visit our group on campus. I was elated, as were the other leaders of the BSU. To think that the Black Panthers were interested in visiting us. I later discovered, after becoming a part of this strategy myself, that the Party was making a concerted effort to organize and recruit from college campuses. Here they found a surplus of disenchanted, angry, young African Americans desperate for an identity and direction.

Very soon after receiving our acceptance to their invitation, the Black Panther contingency from the Denver chapter, one young man and two young women, arrived on our campus. The man spoke for over an hour, flanked by the two ladies, who stood at parade rest the entire time. I don't remember much of what the young man

72

spoke about as he addressed our group, and to be honest, the words didn't seem that important. What impressed me was their demeanor, their obvious strength, and their steely discipline. The two women seemed immobile, never flinching, never moving, staring straight ahead. Outside of a military unit, I had never seen such discipline. These were young African Americans just like us, but they seemed to possess something I didn't—a singlemindedness, a purpose, and a direction. Whatever it was, I knew I wanted it. They seemed to know exactly who they were and where they were going. We all got the impression this group was nothing to be trifled with. They were tough, smart, articulate, and exactly what I aspired to be.

The following weeks and months after that meeting went by quickly, but the impression remained. We continued to deal with racism and inequality on campus and in town, even from other brothers and sisters of color.

In December of 1968, I left Scotts Bluff, Nebraska forever. On our very last day, a group of white football players decided to try and send three of us black students off with a bang. As we walked down the hall of the student union with our bags in hand, we heard the word, "Nigger!" shouted as they closed ranks around us. I don't remember who threw the first punch, but I do remember my friend Howard, a tight end on the college football team, knocking one of them clean off his feet. Howard, who went on to play professional football in Canada, was a very large human being. Between the three of us, the group of five or six football players sorely regretted their actions that day.

We left Hiram Scott College and Scotts Bluff on that day in 1968, never to look back. Hiram Scott College lasted only a short while longer before folding in bankruptcy. When I heard the news, I didn't shed a tear.

THE PANTHER HEADQUARTERS

After bouncing around at several odd jobs on the East Coast, my friends and I, André and Howard, decided to head for California. Howard's sister was a grad student at UC Berkeley, and according to him she had agreed to let the three of us crash at her pad for a short while. However, when we arrived in Berkeley, his sister informed us she had no knowledge of this arrangement, but granted us three nights at her place sleeping on the floor. Fortunately, we had just enough money to get a very cheap apartment in East Oakland.

The San Francisco East Bay was like being on another planet to a young man born and raised on the East Coast. Wandering around Berkeley, California was like being in Disneyland to me, even though I'd never been there either. The city was flooded with hippies and young college students. I'd never seen anything like it. People wore some of the weirdest outfits with tassels, bells, and all sorts of stuff I'd never seen anyone wear—moccasins and coonskin caps and beads everywhere. A lot of the girls were barefoot and half-naked (not that I minded so much).

I was standing on a street corner near University and Telegraph Road when a young man came up and started talking to me. Being from the big city on the East Coast, this was something I wasn't used to. Someone walking up to you on the street usually meant trouble—big trouble—so I was immediately on guard. The dude asked my name and where I was from. To a person raised in a different environment, those questions can seem rather normal, benign even, but to me it felt like what dudes on the street back home would do to someone fresh off the bus from the country (naive, a chump) to distract them while their crime partner was behind him lifting his bags and everything he owned.

My defenses went up immediately. The guy didn't look like he had a tough bone in his body, but you never knew. Many a drifter looked totally harmless, but then, before you knew it, your pockets were empty and you were standing there wondering what had just happened.

His next question was to ask where I was staying, which didn't help my suspicion any. Next, he offered to smoke some hash with me. I was sure he was a narc, but the next thing he said threw me completely. He said if I didn't have any place to stay, I could crash at his pad. This guy was a complete and total stranger. I didn't know him from Adam, and he was offering me the world. Much later in my self-defense seminars, I'd teach participants to be aware of "unnecessary kindness"—a technique used by predators to distract their potential victim, create a false bond, and get the target to quickly trust them. But right before I began to rain blows down on this fellow, I realized this poor soul was high out of his mind and acting just like the hippies I had heard about before coming to Berkeley. Taking a closer look at him, it was obvious he was just living his lifestyle and meant no harm. He really was just being kind. However, I still didn't trust him and walked away, glancing over my shoulder every few feet as I moved on down the street. This was all upside down for me, like having an alien encounter of the third kind.

Here I was, in California, in the heart of the territory of the original Back Panthers. I was still carrying the powerful memory of those young Panthers from Denver, with their military-like discipline and obvious commitment to the cause! It took a few weeks for me to get the courage up, but I soon found myself standing in front of Black Panther National Headquarters in West Oakland. I came in with knees knocking. These were the same people who followed the Oakland police around until it resulted in a shootout that left Bobby Hutton, the Panther's treasurer and very first recruit, lying dead in the street. This was the same group that marched into the California state capital with weapons drawn (though unloaded) to make one of the most aggressive, gutsy, and impactful political statements ever made by any African American group in modern times.

I knew once I crossed the threshold and signed on with the Party that becoming a part of the 20th Century American Revolution was no longer going to be rhetoric. It was going to be real, and there would be no turning back. The Panthers were deadly serious, powerful, and organized. They were also known throughout the black community for their free breakfast programs, free private schools, legal aid assistance, and more—a side never revealed by the press. I wonder how things may have worked out differently if they had. Regardless, these young brothers and sisters were "in it to win it" and had no "back down" in them.

After a short interview with a young Panther official, I was sent to another location in West Oakland to receive my orders. Upon arriving, I soon learned that this Panther base was run by Elmer "Geronimo" Pratt. Geronimo was a young ex-Green Beret in his late twenties who carried himself with supreme confidence. You could tell he had seen and witnessed things most men would shrink from. Geronimo Pratt was a leader to be respected and followed, and I willingly did both. Additionally, he brought a knowledge of the inner workings of US military and our country's intelligence agencies that was invaluable for Panther security. Many of our members had served in the military and had gained valuable experience, but Geronimo's Green Beret background was said to have been above and beyond what most experienced during their service.

My immediate assignment was to sell Black Panther newspapers, which I did faithfully for several months until I was bored stiff. I wanted more. I didn't know if I wasn't trusted or just hadn't earned the right or if that was all there was for me right then, but I had to be involved with more or find some other avenue to be effective.

Shortly after these feelings of restlessness and frustration arose in me, a young female Party member asked me to consider moving into Panther headquarters on a permanent basis. The proposition interested me but made me pause at the same time. I longed to be "in the mix," but I also knew that Panther leadership was not playing games or fooling around. Around the country, Party members were being killed on a regular basis, so moving into Party international headquarters meant being at the command center of the revolution. It meant full commitment to the Party's vision, and believing that vision was vital to the survival of African Americans in this country. It was a vision many were dying for. I did a deep inner search to see if I was ready for this, because if I wasn't, I was not about to dishonor the memory of those who had sacrificed so much for freedom by only giving a partial commitment. There was no room for middle ground; I had to be either in or out.

The Panthers were the most heavily monitored anti-government group in America in the late 1960s. I had no doubt that I had already been identified and catalogued as an associate of the Party but living on Panther premises would elevate me into a whole new category. Was I ready for this step? Would I honor those before me who had sacrificed so much? Was I up to the task? What this meant for my immediate future, I had no idea, but I pondered these questions for a few days and then made my decision.

Until now, I had been showing up at the base pretty regularly—five to six days per week. I'd pick up twenty or thirty newspapers and make my contribution to the cause by spreading the Black Panther Party message of freedom and independence to a community that was becoming more radicalized every day. I was allowed to keep what I sold, which helped me to eat and provide other basic necessities (that along with an occasional care package from home), but not much more. Moving in would change my status from an associate of the Party to a full member, fully committing to the Panther goals and ideology. I agreed.

Soon after moving into the Panther national headquarters in West Oakland, I found myself assigned to the Black Panther newspaper publishing crew. Finally, I was doing something I felt was essential. I worked on the newspaper for several weeks doing menial tasks. It was interesting at first and made me feel like I was providing a vital service to the cause. I was no longer selling papers but was now actually helping to produce the paper.

However, even this duty soon lost its charm and appeal. Many nights when production went into the wee hours of the morning, I slept on the floor in the kitchen of Party headquarters. The gas oven provided the only heat available, and I realized that one day I could wake up dead. I was becoming disillusioned. Had I made a mistake coming to California? Was I ever going to feel at home and satisfied with my current situation in the Panthers?

CHAPTER 8

MERRITT COLLEGE

Feeling a little discouraged, I decided to go back to school. I didn't mind school, and as a matter of fact, I felt that if I could study what I wanted with decent professors, I could enjoy it. I wasn't giving up on the movement or the Panthers; I just felt like I needed something fresh to sink my teeth into.

I'd heard there were good loans available to students. And, after conferring with a couple of counselors at Merritt College on Grove Street in Oakland (one named Tommy became a very close friend), I discovered that these loans would not only cover books and tuition, but if managed well, could provide for some of my living expenses. This, coupled with a student job on campus, could be what I was looking for.

I enrolled and focused in the area of African American studies (Merritt was one of the first colleges to offer such curriculum). I was going to educate myself and really know what I was talking about when it came to the African American experience throughout history and not just in recent US history. In one move, I was going to get an education, which would certainly make Mom and Dad happy, and would achieve a means to support myself. I was very excited and honestly, felt hopeful.

Being back in the academic environment, I thrived. While attending classes and working various part-time jobs, I began to make new like-minded friends, people near my age who were tired of the status quo and wanted to see change sooner rather than later.

Merritt was a lively environment, a beehive of activity. Rallies championing radical causes were frequent: women's rights rallies, impromptu Black Muslim speeches, and "get out the vote" rallies, just to name a few. After all, this was the school the founders of the Black Panther Party had attended. Huey P. Newton and Bobby Seal had walked these halls, and this school was known as the birthplace of the BPP. Herbie Hancock and other famous musicians, poets, and artists had either attended Merritt or were frequent visitors. It was a hotbed of radical thought and fervor.

But one thing was missing: there was no one group representing the average, young African American who wanted an identity of their own but was not interested in joining a theocracy. There was a lot of rhetoric and interesting discussions in class and out on the quad, but no organization. There wasn't even a Black Student Union. When I discovered this, I was surprised. How was it possible that this campus, of all the radicalized campuses in 1969, had no Black Student Union? A little research revealed that there had been one, but it had not survived.

It seemed all too obvious what needed to be done. All this revolutionary fervor needed to be harnessed, focused, and directed. The volcanic heat of Merritt College's angry, young African American student body needed to be funneled into an organized symphony of militant action. I knew I had just the team to lead all this raw potential. It was going to take courage, vision, and smarts, but I was sure we could do it.

The Merritt College Black Student Union was not going to be your average campus BSU. Remember where we were located, in the heart of Oakland, California, the birthplace of the Black Panther Party. Its international headquarters was just a few blocks away. If we organized this group of campus radicals, they would be a force to be reckoned with. Merritt's BSU would be a dangerous organization.

By now, I was associated with some of the strongest, smartest, most courageous individuals I have ever met. We had all met and bonded in such a short period of time that it seemed almost purposeful. For what purpose I did not know, but it was as if something was guiding the process, and there was no coincidence about it.

My good friend from my hometown, André "Dré" Russell, had joined me in California and was enrolled in classes. Though we didn't know each other before Nebraska, we had become close friends while going to school there. Dré was a very intelligent and charismatic young man, easygoing but tough as nails. As a friend, I knew I could entrust him with my life and did so many times over the years. He was one of this mighty band of brothers.

The next was the counselor I mentioned, Tommy Reed, a local guy a few years older than the rest of us. Tommy was a born leader and strong as a bull. I've known professional and elite athletes in many sports over the years, but I've never met a man as physically strong as Tommy, nor one as dedicated to his family. Tommy stood about five-foot-seven or eight and was about two-hundred-fifteen pounds with a barrel chest and a full beard. He had worked as a steel worker for a construction company in the past and was a famous figure amongst high-rise construction steel workers. He was most known for his ability to carry two steel construction beams, one on each shoulder, as he navigated on girders many stories above the streets of San Francisco. Tommy had injured his back and was now employed as an eligibility worker for the college.

Paul Fleming was a very interesting young African American from Virginia. Paul was as bright as anyone I've ever met. He was small in stature and had scoliosis of the spine that created a very noticeable limp and a twist to his back. Though a small man, Paul was game for anything and always had the backs of his comrades.

Next was Joe Stephens. Joe stood six-foot-four and was an imposing figure. He was local, like Tommy, and was well known in the community for his toughness and intelligence.

John Satterwhite, or "Sac" as we called him, was another member. Sac was about five-foot-eleven but was as wide as a freight train and had muscle on top of muscle. He was one of the most feared men on the streets of Oakland and Berkeley.

Last but not least was Tommy Davenport. Tommy was about six-foot-two. He was the best athlete in the group and was built like it. He had been a track star in high school and excelled in most pick-up sports we played. Tommy ultimately forfeited his life for the cause.

This was my crew. We were all highly respected on campus, in the Oakland/Berkeley Community, and by the leadership of the Black Panther Party. I had participated with the Party for several months by now, and the local guys had reputations and strong street cred.

Our first order of business was to get a faculty sponsor and apply for recognition from the college as an official group on campus. My Swahili professor agreed to be our sponsor, and the paperwork was filed. Within a week we received our answer. The organization was now the officially recognized Black Student Union of Merritt

College and assigned a modular hut on campus. I was appointed as the first president of the BSU, Tommy R. vice president, André secretary/treasurer, and Sac was our first sergeant-at-arms. Many others joined us as time passed, but these guys were the core of the BSU and pretty much my life.

In addition to our office on campus, we received permission from a neighborhood church to use one of their unoccupied buildings several blocks from the college on Grove Street. This building was called the Black Church, was painted black, and was a community landmark.

We championed every student-based cause we could find. We focused mainly on the issues affecting black students, of course, but to us race didn't matter. If you were a Merritt College student, we were behind you. We established several free, but well run and well supervised, community-based programs to benefit Merritt College students living in one of the poorest areas of Oakland. We offered a breakfast program that fed seventy to eighty children Monday through Friday, a daycare program, a free clothing program, a small scholarship fund, a used book exchange, and much more. We were completely unlicensed, unauthorized, and probably ill-equipped to do any of this, but we had heart, commitment, passion, smarts, and love for the community we served.

Though the BSU was formed to champion the causes of Merritt's students, one cause became its primary focus in very short order— the move to relocate the campus. Merritt College was a two-year community college located on Grove Street in the heart of West Oakland. As I stated earlier, it was the home of many of the East Bay's finest. Many a talented individual had been educated, trained, and equipped at Merritt and were now having a significant impact in society. The idea to move the college to the Hills of Oakland, a more affluent part of the city, may have made sense to those on the community college school board, but we saw it as a near-criminal act designed to take one of the few major resources we possessed out of our community's reach. Merritt College was a landmark. It was synonymous with Oakland, as much as the Oakland A's or the Oakland Raiders. This school provided members of the West Oakland community a viable way out of the socioeconomic vice grip that had entrapped them for generations. It was a body blow, a slap in the face to the entire, already increasingly disenfranchised, community.

The proposed new site for the college was a one-hour, forty-five-minute bus ride from its current location. It required two bus transfers to complete the trip from the Grove Street campus, and for a young, single parent trying to keep his or her family together and receive an education, it was an impossibility. It meant three hours of travel time, excluding wait times for the first bus to arrive, which also meant three hours of unaffordable, not to mention unavailable, childcare.

The community of West Oakland was in an uproar. Meetings were organized, passionate speeches were given, and petitions were written and signed. Celebrities were solicited and the media alerted, but still plans for the new campus went on as planned. The community college board didn't budge and soon began to break ground for the new campus.

We were probably very naïve about governmental process and how things really got done in those days, but this only added to our feeling powerless and voiceless. Tension was rising, and it seemed to the poor and disenfranchised members of our community that the only time they were heard was when threats were attached to their demands.

Soon, petitions lead to protests. With media in attendance and the whole country watching, a student takeover of the campus was staged. The siege of Merritt College lasted three days, and during that three-day period, the president of the college and all college officials and staff were escorted off campus. The college was completely encircled by thousands of students and community activists, and protestors occupied every office. The campus was locked down.

As often happens in these situations, violence soon erupted. The police came out in force, with dozens of officers in riot gear surrounding the protestors, who had been peacefully protesting up to this point. The police gave every indication that they were ready to clear the campus. Neither the protestors nor their leaders gave an inch. The police advanced against the crowds, batons swinging and boots kicking, while police and news helicopters swirled and dipped overhead. The next several minutes were pure chaos. During the ensuing melee, two protestors were killed and scores injured. The siege took a full day to complete, and in the end the protest leaders were all arrested and carted off to jail, myself included. When Oakland SWAT stormed the college president's office, they found me sitting at his desk. The three-day battle was over.

Despite the outcome, some good did arise from all of this. First, the Alameda Community College school board agreed to leave a satellite campus at the original Grove Street location. Second, the community learned that they did have a voice if they banded together. With these two things accomplished, we felt that we had been somewhat successful, though at great costs.

After spending the night in jail, the three main leaders of the Merritt College takeover appeared before an Alameda County Superior Court judge along with another very effeminate fellow none of us knew or had ever heard of. This unfortunate guy had been walking down the street in San Francisco, several miles across the San Francisco Bay, when the SFPD scooped him up and linked him to us. This poor fellow was totally bewildered and, understandably, scared out of his mind. He looked like the proverbial deer caught in the headlights.

The attorney the Party hired to represent us tried to explain to the Superior Court judge that this fellow was not part of the BSU or the BPP and had no affiliation with any of us or the incidents preceding our arrest. The judge's response was, "Shut up and sit down!" The entire courtroom was stunned. I had never been before a Superior Court judge before, but even to me, this behavior and language seemed to be a bit out of the ordinary to say the least! Miraculously, our lawyer was able to get us all released under our own recognizance (OR). We were stunned. I, for one, had expected to have the book thrown at us. We had a court date to reappear before the judge, but other than that we were free.

Though our lawyer managed to get us an OR, we had little confidence in him. I won't embarrass him here by stating his name (I'm not sure he is even still alive), but his reputation was not very good. He was not respected in the community and apparently not very well respected in the courts either, at least not by that judge. However, Huey Newton, the Black Panther Party's leader and founder, made it clear that we were going to have to make the best of it with this guy. The Party was not going to go deep into its pockets to get a high-priced lawyer to handle our case, so with several charges facing us, we bolted.

In retrospect, this was probably a bad idea. Having been released on OR was an indicator that our case was not being taken very seriously by the judicial system. The District Attorney will often throw several felonies against a defendant at the beginning, knowing that most of them won't stick. However, I could have been an exception since

I was the leader and was in the college president's office when SWAT broke through. We were young and unsophisticated in legal matters of any importance and felt pretty much on our own with an incompetent lawyer and no resources at our disposal. The Party and my comrades were my family, and, with the exception of my fellow defendants, they felt very distant. So, we disappeared.

We later heard that the fellow arrested with us did return to court and was released after the police realized he was not who they thought he was. How they ever did in the first place, I have no clue. He was probably traumatized for life. Can you imagine an average citizen walking down the street minding his own business and suddenly being swooped down upon by the police with guns drawn, spending the night in jail, transported out of your hometown to another county, and set before an obviously irate judge after being accused of being a radical Black Panther revolutionary? And, on top of all that, no one will believe you or even listen to you? These were crazy times, uncharted territory for all of us, but for this fellow it must have been totally surreal.

CHAPTER 9

SAN FRANCISCO COUNTY JAIL

I was in a state of limbo. For the first time in many months, I didn't have a cause to champion. Merritt College was closed down and roped off, and there was no way to get back on campus. After drifting around for a few days, word got to me that the Oakland police and FBI were looking for me. Warrants for my arrest were out for the kidnapping of a state official, assault against a number of individuals, burglary, trespass, and more. Friends picked up by police reported that my picture was posted on the dashboards of both the Berkeley and Oakland Police department's patrol cars.

I suddenly was very popular. Even the FBI was involved. Many of my friends were interviewed and detained. I guess I was fortunate to be currently homeless. I knew if I stayed in the Bay Area I would eventually be apprehended. I seemed to have two choices—either to turn myself in and face the same judge who obviously hated my lawyer and me, or to run. The thought of facing that judge with a less than competent lawyer under those charges was not very appealing, and getting a fair trial was out of the question, so I decided to run.

I managed to spend an entire year deeply underground, basically ceasing to exist for all practical purposes in mainstream society.

Today we call it "living off the grid." During this period in history, disappearing was not a particularly difficult thing to do. In the late sixties and early seventies there were many organizations operating in the US. All were militant and prepared to fight and use weapons. Some established underground networks for dissidents across America and internationally. In the US, some of the players that may have had their own underground networks were the Weather Underground, the Black Liberation Army (BLA), the Brown Berets, the American Indian Movement (AIM), and Black Muslims. Whether or not these groups had their own underground networks is pure speculation on my part, but these groups were known to be radical and violent in self-defense of their platforms. Some sources believed that the BLA and other groups were comprised mostly of ex-Panthers, ex-military, and others. For obvious reasons, I'm not going to write about what I may have done or who may have assisted me in becoming invisible, untraceable, and completely undetected with the intent to avoid arrest. However, I was later accused of being a cadre leader in the Black Liberation Army, the same position I held in the BPP.

Early one morning in June of 1971, a few comrades and I were sleeping in a second-floor tenement flat in San Francisco when the front and back doors exploded simultaneously, and bulletproof vested police officers and FBI agents came through with drawn assault weapons, shotguns, and pistols. Chaos and confusion erupted as orders were barked out and objects flew around the room. Three of us were arrested that day: my good friend Paul, another fellow I'll call Wendell, and myself.

I'm not sure of all the charges that were levied against the other two, but according to my lawyer, the charges pending against me were treason against the United States government, attempted bombing of the South African embassy, kidnapping of a state official, assault, and a laundry list of other charges I don't remember and that had no consequence after reading the first three or four. I don't remember being arraigned, but our lawyer says I was. As a matter of fact, I don't remember ever leaving the seventh floor of the Bryant Street building, where the jail was housed, until I was released into State of California custody.

During interrogations by federal agents, I learned that they suspected we had been all over the United States executing acts of sabotage as members of the BLA. One other interesting fact was that the US attorney told our lawyer that J. Edgar Hoover, Director of the Federal Bureau of Investigation (FBI) himself, was personally monitoring our case. The hole we were in seemed very deep and very, very dark.

The federal government had a contract with San Francisco County to house their prisoners on the seventh floor of their Bryant Street facility. Federal prisoners were, as a rule, mixed in with the general population in large cells containing masses of inmates, unless you were considered "high-profile." Paul and Wendell were put in the general population, but I was treated like a rock star and put on a cellblock that housed no other prisoners. The other cells were completely empty.

My mind was in a complete fog, partially due to malnutrition. While on the run from the authorities, good home-cooked meals were very hard to come by. For a year, I had only eaten fast food or quick snacks when available. I had never been a big guy, but at the time of my arrest I was five-foot-eleven and weighed a generous hundred-and-thirty-five pounds.

The first twenty-four hours after our arrest seemed like a dream. It was all so surreal. I kept thinking I'd wake up any minute, but of course I didn't. Alone, in total isolation on that empty cellblock, I was cold, both in physical temperature and in spirit. I later found out that this section of the jail had been closed for repairs. Amongst the repairs were the environmental control units that controlled the heat and cooling. So, no heat for me. I'd always preferred the warmer weather of the East Bay to the cold dampness of San Francisco and the West Bay. It was kind of ironic that I'd wind up in the coldest section of a jail in San Francisco.

I was also physically and spiritually isolated, and the silence was deafening. When someone did enter the block, the sudden intrusion of harsh sounds made by metal doors clanging and loud voices was worse than any alarm clock you could imagine. It was as if every cell in my body awoke and came to stark attention. To further exacerbate the emptiness of this cold, drafty place, the tier above me on the second level was also totally empty. I had read all about overcrowded jails teeming with humanity, but two empty cellblocks just for me? Of course, I was relieved to not have masses of people to deal with. I was weak, malnourished, and disoriented.

The federal holding facility located on the seventh floor was real jail, where inmates from Folsom, San Quentin, and other places, were held as well. I'm not saying it was the same as the penitentiary, but it was as close as I'd ever come. Up until now I'd only experienced staying overnight in a local police facility. This, however, was the real deal.

For several days, I was alone in that cell; trustees served all the meals. I started a rigorous exercise routine that consisted of hundreds of military pushups, sit-ups, deep knee-bends, and other calisthenics to gain weight and strength. I only left for an occasional shower. Unfortunately, the pushups exacerbated a torn rotator cuff I had incurred playing high school football. It became inflamed, causing me more pain than I had ever experienced in my life. The prison doctor examined me and requested that I be moved to an outside hospital but was informed that I was too high a security risk and he would have to make do with what he had in the infirmary to treat me.

Soon, someone was brought in on the tier above me. From interactions between this new inmate and guards, I soon discovered that this person was an inmate from San Quentin, Ruchell Magee. Magee had been arrested in the infamous Marin County Courthouse shootout during an attempt to free George Jackson, a Black Panther and San Quentin inmate, during the trial of another Panther named James McClain. General George, as he was known throughout Black Panther circles and to the radical community, was a Panther leader who had been incarcerated for a number of years for stealing a seventy-dollar television set. He didn't go into prison a Panther but became one inside. Magee was called to testify as a witness at McCain's trial. The plan of the assault team had been to capture hostages during the trial and use them as leverage to free Jackson. George Jackson's younger brother Jonathan was killed during the attempt, along with James McClain, Superior Court judge Harold Haley, and Panther William Christmas. Others were gravely wounded. This is the incident that made Angela Davis famous, as she was sought as an accomplice and later arrested.

Though I was excited to have another human to interact with, Ruchell Magee was having none of it. He wouldn't talk at all. I assumed he was leery of this supposed fellow Panther conveniently housed on the tier right below where there was not another living human being. After so many years in prison and all he had been through recently, I figured he had the right to be skeptical of anyone he did not know or even people he did. Slowly the tier began to be populated, but before I could get to know anyone, I was taken from isolation into the lion's den.

THE BLACK PANTHER AND THE FOLSOM NAZI

One evening about two weeks after I'd been arrested, two guards came, opened my cell, and ordered me to gather my possessions. This was quite easy to do, since the only thing I owned was what I was arrested in, the boots I was wearing, and my underwear. From this isolated tier I was taken to D-block, which I soon discovered was where all the bad boys were housed.

This cellblock had about six cells in it, a large four-man cell just inside the cellblock gate and a four-man shower at the end of the tier. The remaining cells consisted of two-man cells.

The guards took me to the second cell in the row, and when the cell door opened, I could hardly believe my eyes. What I saw was the largest swastika on the back of one of the largest white men I had ever seen. As the cell door closed behind me, I heard the guards snicker, and one said out loud, "It's gonna be an interesting night." I don't know whose idea it was to put me in the same cell with a Nazi, but whoever it was had to know that putting a professing Nazi and a Black Panther and accused Black Liberation Army cadre leader in a small cell together created a very volatile situation that would likely end in violence, serious injury to one of us, and/or possibly death. This indeed was going to be a very interesting night.

My new cellmate was obviously occupying the bottom bunk, so I quickly jumped up to the top one. He didn't even turn to look at me, and I didn't know what to think as I sized up this monster of a man with the gigantic swastika. He was standing in front of the only sink in the cell and was so wide you couldn't see an inch of the sink while standing behind him. He completely dwarfed any view of what was on the other side of his body.

I probably slept a total of thirty minutes that night. I sat upright with my back against the wall behind me and never took my boots off. The only weapons I had were my hands and feet, and I quickly decided that my feet would be a great deal more deadly with my hard wooden-heeled boots still in place than my hands. I was determined that if my new "celly" made any kind of move on me during the night, he'd have to fight his way past a barrage of boot heels and knuckles. I knew deep down that an attack was inevitable, but it never came.

The next morning, I met the man that would become my closest friend over the next several months. My new cellmate's name was Blink. Just Blink. Blink stood about six-foot-one and weighed about two-hundred-and-sixty-five pounds. In a small two-man cell, his size was daunting. He was massive. Blink had twenty-inch biceps and a waist that was about thirty-four inches. He was chiseled to say the least and was known in prison jargon as a "hog." On farms, hogs are huge, stubborn, ornery, mean, extremely strong animals, and will eat and attack anything. This man was in his mid-thirties and had spent a great deal of his youth and his whole adult life in prison. It was clear he had spent most of that time in the weight yard. The swastika taking up the entirety of his back indicated that he was a dedicated member of the Arian Brotherhood. He was a formidable and intimidating man to say the least.

In the morning, Blink spoke two words: "What's up?"

"What's up!" I answered.

On D-block, inmates ate in their cells. Breakfast came—a lovely serving of porridge, milk, and bread—and we ate in silence. That was breakfast pretty much every morning, unless you wanted water.

D-block inmates consisted of federal prisoners awaiting trial or hardcore state prison inmates who had committed serious crimes in one of Northern California's state prisons and were also awaiting trial. Most infractions in state prison were adjudicated in the prison itself. To be taken to an outside state court meant the crime committed had to be very serious, such as escape or attempted escape, serious injury to another inmate up to and including murder, or injuring prison staff.

I soon discovered that Blink was no longer a member of the Arian Brotherhood and had renounced their beliefs and practices. While doing a stint in San Quentin, Blink heard George Jackson speak and was fascinated. He'd never heard words of unity and anti-racism while incarcerated. Blacks hated whites, and they both hated the Mexicans and vice versa. It was just an accepted way of life in prison. You joined a set or you got "punked."

Blink continued to hear George's teachings whenever he could get away with it, which I imagined was not easy. Being courageous, he actually approached George to learn more. I never met George Jackson, but I did know his family and had read his writings. I knew enough about him to know that he probably saw this as an opportunity to breach the racial divide. George was not a racist. He saw racism as a tactic to keep the races divided and separated. George was an American revolutionary who believed the only way to effect lasting change was to unify all the races into one force. He believed there is strength in numbers.

George Jackson befriended Blink and convinced him that blacks, whites, Hispanics, Asians, and other races fighting each other was a waste of human effort towards no good end. It accomplished nothing but division and perpetual hatred between races for no rational reason. George believed, like most of us at the time, that the real war was against class oppression and the "haves" against the "have-nots."

Blink was aware of my case and why I was incarcerated with him, and he proved to be quite intelligent and well read. He told me that General George held daily "study sessions" and had taught Blink much about social issues, class struggle, Marxism, dialectical materialism, and much more. We very quickly became friends and soon developed a close bond. We also had a good laugh over how the guards who put us together had to be so disappointed that the fireworks they expected never materialized

CHAPTER 10

LIVING IN A CAGE

Weeks went by, and I learned how to conduct myself in this new environment. I learned that there was a strict code in jail. A man's word was his bond and meant everything. Once you broke your word, you were labeled and rarely, if ever, were trusted by your fellow inmates again. Strangely enough, honesty was extremely important. A jailhouse thief was almost as low as a snitch. Pedophiles were the lowest and were often marked for death. Courage was highly regarded, as was a man who could defend himself. I also learned, or relearned, pig Latin. It was used to communicate in code, and I was amazed to discover how many people couldn't speak it since I had learned it as a kid. I was also taught Gaelic! I'm not trying to glorify life in jail but to paint a picture for those readers who may have no idea what life is like behind bars, at least the way it was in the early 1970s. Blink was a good acquaintance to make for a number of reasons.

I shared a cell with Blink for several weeks until I moved to another cell to make room for a new prisoner fresh in from Folsom. This new inmate's name was Al, and he was a good friend of Blink's. Al was black but not affiliated with any group I knew of. Somewhere during their incarceration together in San Quentin and Folsom, Blink and Al had become good friends, so I moved to a spot two cells down. The move wasn't a complete sacrifice for leaving my new friend because now I had a cell to myself.

Al was a different animal. He was short but almost as muscular as Blink and loved to show off his strength by doing inverted pushups (upside down) against the wall. He was also a "hog" and a total predator preying on anything weak in the most bestial ways. Very few people were safe around him, including me. An atmosphere of violence and danger permeated the air in his presence, and if he sensed that you were in the least intimidated you became a target and possibly his next victim.

Al's demeanor was completely different around Blink. You could hear them laughing and joking far into the night in their cell. Blink disagreed with Al on just about everything, but there was an undeniable bond between them. I got the feeling that they had been through a few wars together. They appeared to be brothers-in-arms, warriors forged in the crucible of some unknown combat, though they were as different as night and day.

Al didn't know what to make of me. I was becoming stronger every day and was doing seven hundred pushups a day to pack on size and muscle as fast as I could, though I was still only about a hundred-forty-five pounds soaking wet. Al hadn't witnessed the physical progress I had made and did not know about nor care about my political exploits or infamy. To him I was this skinny runt of a guy who should have been prey in there. He knew Blink respected me but didn't know why.

One night I could hear them whispering, and though I could not understand much of what they were saying, I got a sinking feeling in my stomach. I was sure they were talking about me. More specifically, Al was talking about me. I had seen predatory glances clandestinely directed my way in the shower and felt a bloody confrontation was sure to come.

Suddenly I heard Blink say, just loud enough for his voice to carry down two cells, "Greg"—one of the many aliases I was using when arrested that stuck for a long time—"is no punk, Al. You'd be making a mistake trying him."

I know it sounds crazy, but it was one of the proudest moments of my young life. I had been tested many times by bullies and alpha males. I was a runt, had a pretty mellow, easy-going demeanor, and was supposed to be easy prey. Most of the time the tester got a response he wasn't expecting. On one occasion a high-ranking leader of the Black Panther Party found that out when he, for no apparent reason, tried to intimidate me into giving him a personal item of mine. He was surrounded by three bodyguards and was pretty big himself. He continued to press me, but the more he pressed the more I resisted, until one of his buddies nicknamed "Big Man" reminded him I was the brother who effectively removed a very disturbed young dude when he initiated a physical confrontation with Huey Newton the day Huey was released from prison.

Kathleen Cleaver, the wife of Eldridge Cleaver, a former UC Berkeley professor and the Panther's Minister of Education, witnessing this exchange between this Panther official and I, commented to me afterward that I had more heart than brains.

That endorsement from Blink went a long way. I never got a sniff of malevolence from Al again, and as a matter of fact, Blink, Al, and I soon formed a triad. Blink was doing life in prison; he was very quiet but very dangerous. Al was doing life in prison, as well; he was quite boisterous and verbose and also was very dangerous. I was facing life or worse and became our mouthpiece. I also was becoming more dangerous every day as I grew bigger and stronger. I was on a regime of seven or eight hundred pushups a day, plus other body-building exercises. I was also being tutored and prepared for prison life by these two every day.

Then, one day, I got a new cellmate. His name was Phillip Tucker. Phillip was a little younger than me, about twenty years old, slim but athletic and quite strong. He had been in the penitentiary since he was sixteen years old. George Jackson had taken Phillip under his wing, trained him in the martial arts, and had eventually made him a lieutenant in his prison organization. I found a kindred spirit in Phillip and became close friends with this very charismatic young inmate almost instantly. Phillip loved to laugh and was full of life.

George had trained him well, and he was near black-belt level in skill. He and I trained daily, much to the intense interest of other inmates and the chagrin of the jail staff. Our training was very hard: hundreds of pushups and calisthenics daily, sparring, training our fists against the concrete walls. I was still gaining weight and was now about a hundred-fifty-five pounds of lean muscle. All of this was done out in the open for all to see. There was no privacy, and our two-man cells were way too small for the type of rigorous training we were subjecting our bodies to, but for two slim young men it was necessary to survive in this environment.

There was an incident when all my training, while incarcerated and before, served me well. One morning, a large group of prisoners were being transported to court. Wendell, whom I had not seen since we had been apprehended, and I were included in the bunch. One of the guards the prisoners called Hercules was giving my friend, Wendell, a hard time. Hercules was a Nazi. He and a few other guards who were also Nazis would manipulate their schedules, so they would be the only staff on duty during some of the night shifts.

When no other staff officials were on duty to see, they would all don their swastika armbands.

Hercules was abusing Wendell needlessly—pushing him, prodding him with his baton, and provoking him into a possible confrontation. We were all shackled together with leg chains, and I was several places behind Wendell witnessing the whole thing. To my chagrin, Wendell was being very passive, allowing Hercules to push him, abuse him, and make him appear weak. I had no idea what sort of indignities Wendell may have suffered since being incarcerated, but this display in front of so many did not bode well for him.

I spoke up and demanded he be left alone. I was possibly facing the death penalty for treason and was sure to be found guilty, so I figured I had nothing to lose.

Hercules wanted to know who was doing the protesting. I identified myself and demanded he leave my friend alone since he wasn't doing anything in violation of the house rules. Hercules and his partner, who was nicknamed "Deputy Dog" because of his exceptionally long ears and facial features (he looked like the horse cartoon character), approached me. They asked me if I was looking for trouble, to which I replied, "No, no trouble. Just leave him alone." Hercules asked if I wanted to take his place. I stated that if he took the chains off of my legs, I'd be happy to properly introduce myself. We glared at each other for a few seconds before he turned away, but he left with a promise that there'd be trouble later. I didn't doubt it.

When I got back from the court hearing (that didn't happen due to a delay), I was immediately stripped and thrown into the "hole." The hole was a ten-by-ten-foot padded room. There was no furniture or bed, only a bench, and you were stripped totally naked. There were no toilet facilities, but there was a hole in the floor for the occupant's convenience. The guards controlled the flushing of the hole from outside, and every time they flushed it, waste would back up onto the floor, frequently ankle deep. There was no washbasin.

That night, I had visitors. I could hear them outside my space talking and planning who was going in first, talking and swearing, getting their courage up. While they were getting ready, I prepared myself. I decided my best strategy was to not fight back unless I thought I had to in order to survive.

I got into a horseback-riding stance (a taekwondo training stance that is not threatening like a fighting stance would be) and began deep breathing exercises. I began to prepare my mind and body for an attack. While deep breathing, I did my best mind-over body exercise, transforming my body into steel, a rock-hard, metal sculpture that couldn't be harmed.

Then three of them came through the door—Hercules, Deputy Dog, and another Nazi. I immediately noticed the fear on their faces. They were truly cowards, scared of one naked man against three. I knew not one of them would dare face a man alone. Hercules cautiously approached. His lips were moving, but I was focused on his eyes. He was spewing some nonsense about facing the consequences and asking if I thought I was a big man now. I didn't speak at all—no false bravado, no empty promises, just me in my obvious martial arts stance staring silently into his eyes.

He was shaking. I could tell he wanted out of there, but his comrades were watching and expecting...something. So, he gathered himself and threw an upper cut that caught me in my stomach, just below my lowest rib. Hercules was quite short, so it was no surprise that his shot was low. A second before the blow, I tensed and felt nothing. He got no reaction—no cry in pain, no buckling over, no cry for mercy.

To this day, I believe that scared him more than anything.

He attempted another blow to the same area. Nothing. Then a third. By now, I realized something. As buffed and muscle-bound as Hercules was, he had no power! His blows were weak. I learned later that men who over-train with weights and overdevelop certain muscle groups sacrifice striking power. He could have picked me up with one hand and thrown me all over that padded room if he had chosen, but his punches had no effect at all. The look on his face was priceless.

Anticipating that this encounter could easily escalate into something I couldn't safely come back from, I answered a quiet "yes" to his question if I had learned my lesson. They all slowly backed out of the room, careful not to turn their backs on me, slammed the door shut, and left. My next two days in the hole were uneventful.

On my third or fourth day in, I heard my name being called from the other side of the door. Wendell had also been thrown in the hole next to mine. I had tried to talk to him, but after a short acknowledgement after my first effort to communicate with him, he stopped responding. I could tell it wasn't him calling my name.

I didn't respond. I figured it was the guards calling out my name and if they wanted to talk to me they could very well open the door and come in. At least I'd get a whiff of fresh air and maybe a little sun from a nearby barred, screened, and shaded window. But they didn't come in, and I continued to ignore them.

Then, Hercules (through the cell door) offered to let me take a shower. I couldn't believe it. They kept saying I could shower if I wanted, but I was suspicious. First of all, it was Hercules, who never offered a kindness to anyone, and secondly, they weren't making the same offer to Wendell.

Then they pulled out the big guns and said that my mother was there to see me. My mother? Ridiculous. I knew they were lying, but the offer of a shower was just too good to pass up. If only I could get Wendell to agree to shower as well. I said I would come out and shower if he were allowed to also. We went back and forth, but they finally agreed to let Wendell shower with me.

I called out to him. No answer. Again I called out, still no answer. Didn't he understand that I was in this predicament helping him? Now, I needed backup, and he was acting totally weird. This time I yelled at him, and this time he answered.

"I don't want to shower, man! Leave me alone."

We'd been in this stinking hole for days, and he didn't want to shower? Was he crazy or just totally broken? I didn't know, and I never found out because I never saw Wendell again.

It was against my better judgment, but I just couldn't sit in the filth any longer. I yelled through the door that I would take the shower. As I passed Wendell's cell on the way to the multiple shower room I yelled, "Thanks a lot!" to him. He never replied. Looking back, I can't imagine what he had been made to suffer in there. I believe this man had been totally broken by the Nazi guards or other inmates. Something happened to him, but I'll never know what.

As I entered the shower, one of the guards handed me a bar of soap, a towel, and a bottle of shampoo. Shampoo? Now I knew trouble was coming. Shampoo is not jail issue. Something was up.

I had a huge Afro. I figured their plan was to give me shampoo, have me lather that big 'fro up so that I couldn't see, and then bad things were going to happen. These guys were Class A cowards. It's helpful to be a little bit smarter than your enemy. I took the shampoo, wet my hair, but only applied the shampoo to half of my scalp, leaving me some visibility. This turned out to be a wise decision.

After about two minutes in the shower, just as I was about to shampoo the other side, I heard a voice yelling, "Watch out, Greg! They're rolling on you!"

I wiped my face clear as best I could, prepared to defend my life, and quickly turned to see the library trustee standing in the doorway of the shower, watching as the three Nazis advanced on me—two brandishing axe handles and one a baton. You may say, "I've never seen axe handles carried by guards in any prison movie!" But just remember the movie Cool Hand Luke. Also, remember that this was 1971 and not a movie.

At the sound of the librarian's voice, the Nazis spun as one and spat out a command for him to leave the area. This man owed me nothing, but he knew what they represented and knew why I was incarcerated. I believe he also knew or suspected I was the one smuggling articles to the newspapers regarding these Nazis and the conditions in this hellhole (more to come on these articles later).

The trustee refused to leave. They threatened him again. I will never forget his answer.

"I'm not leaving. You'll have to kill me, too."

I don't remember this man's name, but I do remember he was not a big man. As I recall, he was of medium height and slightly built. His willingness to sacrifice himself for my life was noble, an expression of prison-ethics honor.

The guards hesitated, apparently pondering the predicament they would be in trying to explain the deaths of two inmates. They could possibly explain my murder, as I was known as a violent, dangerous inmate. They could easily say that, while attempting to give me the privilege of a shower, I attacked them and they had no choice but to use weapons against me. Even if I didn't perish, it would be my word against three officers. But two inmates going down in this scenario, one of whom was non-violent and entrusted with the run of the facility, would be hard to explain. They would have to kill us both, or the testimony of either of us would be very damning to their veneer of innocent guards trying to detain a dangerous inmate to defend their lives.

My friend refused to leave, and the three baffled Nazis decided it was better to bide their time and wait for another opportunity. That opportunity came a few short weeks later.

THE POWER OF THE PRESS

I mentioned the newspaper articles. Shortly after my arrest, I started making notes on the things I witnessed in jail, like the notes one would take during a class. I was not writing to anyone in particular; it just helped to pass idle time.

When I told my lawyer about these notes, he asked to see them. I gave them to him without a second thought. He was dating a good friend of mine and I thought perhaps he would share them with her, and she would pass word to other friends and associates of mine that I was surviving and doing okay. What I didn't know was that he started submitting them to a local radical Bay Area newspaper called *The Berkeley Barb*.

There was a large four-man cell at the front end of our cellblock where prisoners who were clearly mentally ill were kept. It was obvious these men did not have the mental capacity to care for themselves. They never showered or submitted their jail uniforms to the laundry, and both inmates and guards victimized them in every way. The stench from their area was so intense you had to cover your nose and mouth as you walked by.

After some time, I started going into their cell and ordering them to change into the clean uniforms the trustees always left for them and place their dirty ones in the pick-up area. I could not get them to shower, but at least changing their clothes and bedding helped with the gagging odor and made me, at least, feel better about their living conditions.

Our meals were a joke. Every morning we were served something unidentifiable I can only describe as mush, a small carton of milk, and one slice of white bread. Lunch was no better—a couple of dry lunchmeat sandwiches and a salad, accompanied by another carton of milk or a cup of water. We had to be careful with that salad. It was straight from the county jail's farm, was barely washed, and often came with a couple of hitchhiking worms. You could expect no meat with dinner. We got meat once a week for dinner—maybe twice if luck was with us. Dinner was mostly starch, noodles, and salad with a slice of white bread. I wrote about all these things in my notes.

I also wrote about the medical care—or rather, lack of care—we received. I was in constant, often excruciating pain from the torn rotator cuff in my left shoulder. The only treatment at the time that helped was a steroid injection. I would not submit to one now, knowing what I now know about the dangers of over-exposure to steroid injections, but at the time that was my only source of relief when the pain was at its peak. The facility's doctor could not prescribe anything stronger than aspirin for the pain. He would give me a couple to take back to my cell, but we both knew it would do nothing to help.

During one of these acute episodes, the pain was so intense the doctor wanted me hospitalized, so I could get the proper treatment and perhaps surgery to repair the tear. The jail administration refused the request, stating I was too high profile a prisoner, and they did not want another escape attempt like the one that had just been attempted with George Jackson.

When the doc informed me of their decision, he was obviously upset and was very compassionate. He saw a person and a patient in need, not a dangerous individual. He appealed the decision and was denied again. Looking back, I can understand the decision. The administrators were dealing with an unprecedented set of circumstances. These revolutionaries seemed to have no fear and no respect for the establishment, and as far as the administrators were concerned they would be putting their personnel in real danger for a prisoner suffering a little shoulder pain. As far as they knew, I could be faking it to get outside the jail and onto the street, where an attempt could be made to free me. After all, I was facing some very daunting charges with very little hope of ever sniffing free air again, compounded by the fact that I had some very dangerous associates on the outside. It's amazing how much each man's perspective can color the same situation such a different way. I was nowhere near George's league, but they weren't taking any chances.

I wrote about this instance in my notes. I also wrote about the activities of our local neighborhood Nazis, Hercules and his cohorts. I wrote it all down.

What I did not know was the facility doctor was so upset about his inability to treat his patients as he wished that he went to *The San Francisco Chronicle* and told it all. *The Chronicle* published his story on the front page, I was told, in a series of articles. I did not have access to newspapers, so I had to take my lawyer's word for it at the time. His exposé created quite a stir in the outside world.

Meanwhile, I had been released from the hole and was back in my cell on D-block. Not knowing any of the events described above were going on, I was becoming more and more agitated about our living conditions. I felt the conditions in the jail were inhuman, and no one outside the walls cared in the least. One day I decided I wouldn't eat in protest. I didn't know what my protest would accomplish, but felt I had to do something, or I would go nuts.

One man not eating didn't cause much of a stir, but to my surprise, the hunger strike caught on with the other inmates—first with Blink, then Al, then Phillip, and soon the whole cellblock. When asked in the common exercise room, I told every man who would listen why I was on strike. I told them I was striking because it wasn't right to have defenseless mentally ill inmates in the same population with high-functioning inmates. I said I was protesting the food, poor medical care, and general overall institutional oversight allowing renegade Nazi guards to roam free in the facility. My words may not have been as polished as they are now, but everyone got the point.

People had seen me taking care of other inmates who couldn't fend for themselves and not taking advantage of them. They had seen me take on the guards in defense of a friend, and they all, by now, knew why I was in there in the first place. I had become a bit of a celebrity and leader. It also didn't hurt I was running with three of the toughest guys on any penitentiary yard.

The strike soon spread to other cellblocks and to the general population units. People weren't eating, and there was concern that word of the protest would get out and bring unwanted attention to the jail, its staff, and inmates. Soon, the jail personnel decided to take action. On the fourth day of the strike, jail personnel started to assemble just outside our cellblock. Heading the group of about five or six officers was my old friend Hercules and one of his sidekicks. This was his chance to have a legitimate shot at revenge, and he was pumped. Wielding axe handles, batons, and an array of weapons, they ordered us to eat the food that had just been delivered on carts outside our cells or face dire consequences.

When I decided to join the Black Panther Party, people were being killed, frequently. I knew I could be one of those people. Friends of mine had sacrificed their lives during that time and during the time the authorities were hunting me, before being arrested in San Francisco. The list included one of my closest friends, Tommy Davenport.

I had never been particularly brave as a kid, though I had my occasional moments. But obtaining equality at all costs was what I had signed up for. Now here it was again. In that moment I had to remind myself what this was all about. Malcolm was dead. Martin was dead. George Jackson and his brother Jonathan were dead. Even JFK and his brother Bobby were dead. The two brothers beaten to death at the Merritt College protest were dead, and most of all, Tommy was dead, along with many others. I was ready and knew it, and amazing myself once again, after a moment I stood up and walked out of my cell.

I walked straight to the cellblock gate. Trying to keep my voice from quivering, I said I wasn't eating until I saw some changes made, and I couldn't be forced to. They looked at each other in silent agreement and started to open the cellblock gate, but before they came through, I saw a beautiful sight from the corner of my eye. I saw the huge hulk that was Blink come out of his cell and stand just behind my left shoulder. I could have kissed him. Of course, that would not have been appreciated. Then to my total surprise, I saw apolitical Al come out and stand just behind my right shoulder. He later stated he couldn't care less about the strike, and had, in fact, been eating the whole time, but couldn't let his comrades go down alone. Finally, Phillip came out and stood behind the other two directly behind me!

Picture this scene: Blink and Al alone probably outweighed four of the guards by themselves and definitely had more muscle, even with Hercules amongst them. These guys were massive. Then there was Phillip and me. I was probably up to about a hundred-sixty pounds by now, but was all muscle. Phillip was tall and slender, but his fighting and martial arts prowess were well known.

There was a momentary standoff. Then, the funniest thing happened. One of the deputies was a black man and was standing on the side of the group, sort of on the fringe. He never had that look in his eye telling you that a man is all-in on what is about to go down. He threw his axe handle down, saying with obvious conviction, "They don't pay me enough to go in there!" He turned and left the scene behind, never looking back.

That started the exodus. One by one, the remaining deputies began to peel away, until only Hercules was left with his sidekick Deputy Dog. You could see the wheels turning in his head, weighing the odds of a successful outcome in his mind. Deputy Dog stood there, staring at his leader. You could see he was standing his ground only out of pure loyalty to his comrade, but his nervous glances and slight shifting from one foot to another belied the fact that he really did not want to come through that gate. He was scared out of his mind. The men facing him had no families to go home to and literally had nothing to lose but more jail time added to life sentences. Sure, they could have been seriously hurt or worse, but they faced those possibilities on a daily basis in prison. Anyway, prison was where they were all headed back to one way or another.

I don't know if it was cowardice or just plain good sense that made them turn away, but with pure hatred in his eyes, Hercules simply turned and walked away with his companion close at his heels. I never saw those two or their other Nazi friend ever again. They were all soon unceremoniously fired from the San Francisco sheriff's department.

SHAKE, RATTLE, AND ROLL

As you know, all of the events I recorded in simple handwritten notes, I eventually put into the hands of my lawyer, Andrew. At the time, I had no idea what Andrew was doing with them. I did find it strange that occasionally after recreation in the common room, I would return to find my bed stripped, and my bedding on the floor with the mattress in a tumbled mess. Likewise, my meager belongings—a notebook, a couple of ballpoint pens my lawyer had given me, a razor, some personal hygiene items, and perhaps a book I was currently reading—would all be lying in a heap on the cell floor, as well as my cellmate's belongings. The guards had evidently come in looking for what, I did not know. At first, I thought it was just spite motivating these seemingly senseless attacks on my simple possessions, but then a trustee and a couple of other inmates reported they had heard the search parties talking about looking for something specific. They heard them say that they were sure I was the source of something unknown. I began to wonder what this something was and what this was all about.

The answer to this mystery came during my next visit with Andrew. He told me what he had done with my notes and the articles that had been published. Now, I knew why my cell had been tossed and what the guards had been looking for. Someone had seen the articles in the little local newspaper popular only with the Bay Area radical set, and had tipped off the jail personnel.

The idea was funny. I couldn't remember half of what I had written and wondered how much editing Andrew had done. Quite a bit, I was sure. I was proud of myself and very surprised at Andrew, as I didn't think he had a radical bone in his body. Though quite laidback and congenial, Andrew was very professional. I figured he was sympathetic to our cause but didn't know he would step up like that, for all the good it would do.

Then, things really got interesting. As I mentioned before, the doctor who was not allowed to treat my shoulder told *The San Francisco Chronicle* everything he knew about the inner workings of the San Francisco County Jail, 7th Floor. *The Chronicle* published it all in a series of articles over two or three days. Then, the newspaper picked up *The Berkeley Barb* stories and re-ran them. What happened next had ramifications throughout the jail.

A Superior Court judge took it upon himself to come into the jail as an inmate. I don't know who knew it and I never saw him, but evidently, he saw plenty. It's not clear how many nights he spent in there, one night or two, it doesn't matter. The end result was the firing of the captain of the jail, the equivalent to a prison warden, and several guards, including Hercules and his crew. Mentally ill inmates were segregated from the general population for their protection, and the food improved markedly (suddenly there was meat every day). I never went back to the infirmary, so I can only assume the medical treatment for inmates received an upgrade, as well.

It was a miracle, and I was a celebrity. The change was so sudden and unexpected, you would have thought that we had been set free. What I remember the most was the upgraded food and the freedom of not having to look at the faces of my archenemies—the Nazi crew. I never heard of any charges filed against them, but I knew they were gone and had been fired with a bunch of others. I took the victory for what it was.

I couldn't believe all this had happened in the space of five months or so; it was very surreal. Jail was anything but boring, and I lived in a constant state of alert, as I believe every inmate does. Don't misunderstand me, please. Most people incarcerated are there for a good reason. There were people in that jail who needed to be isolated from the public. I am just reporting a set of events that helped shape my life, and a period of time that shaped how I saw the world and who I thought I was. I was still heading toward destruction, and I knew it. I knew I had made some friends in county, friends who might help me survive the next few years in whatever federal penitentiary I wound up in, but my future still looked very dark . . . until I heard the voice of God.

CHAPTER 11

WHO ARE YOU?

When you are incarcerated, time seems to move so slowly. I had only been in custody for a few months, but it already felt like years. Given time, all living organisms will adjust to any environment if it's not toxic and can support life; human beings are no exception. Once you realize you have no choice, you adjust, just like a bonsai tree will grow in the direction in which it is being pruned given enough time.

I was beginning to adjust to this life quite well. Other inmates constantly expressed their surprise when they discovered I was not a seasoned veteran of the state penitentiary system. Under the tutelage of Blink, Al, and Phillip, I learned quickly. I observed them closely and learned how to carry myself. From them I learned how to avoid situations (a hard lesson for me—life in there was very different than life in the world), who to befriend, and who not to. I learned to keep my mouth shut when needed and to mean everything I said when I said it. I learned the importance of loyalty, honesty amongst inmates, and standing up in the face of all odds and under incredible pressure.

But now they were all gone. Their cases were resolved, and one by one they returned to prison. Several weeks after the new reforms had begun, life was very different. Several new officers had been brought into the jail. The inmates were getting used to the new guards and their idiosyncrasies as much as they were getting used to ours. In addition to better food, the atmosphere had changed. The overall tension level had been dialed down several notches, which I'm sure had as much to do with my heightened feeling of security as it was due to the reforms being implemented and the more humane attitudes of the new staff. These new guys seemed to have a level of professionalism about them that few of their predecessors had ever possessed. My status in the facility had certainly taken a significant boost. I was now a minor celebrity, whether deserved or not, as word got around about both sets of articles. The undercover judge stated the whole sting operation had been initiated due to the released articles.

Now that my closest allies were gone, I was spending a lot of time alone. D-block was almost empty, and I, once again, had a cell to myself.

One afternoon, our jail librarian came around with his book cart. This was the same brave soul who had shouted the warning and stood up with me when I was about to be attacked in the prison shower by Hercules and his boys. As usual, the cart was all but empty by the time he made his way to D-block. He pulled up with the cart, and we exchanged greetings and the latest news as I searched the near empty cart for something interesting to read that would help hold back the loneliness and boredom and pass the time.

Being alone for those few days was both a blessing and a curse. I was enjoying the quiet most of all and the peace of not having to constantly watch my back. I had freedom to work out on the tier without constant scrutiny from other inmates assessing my strengths and weaknesses, and it made my workouts freer and less self-conscious. On the other hand, loneliness and isolation were starting to feel like a living thing threatening to close in on me. I hadn't been alone that long, but after months of noise, constant activity, and yes, fear, this new experience was a little unnerving.

I had been on a tier alone when I was first brought in, but this felt different. That first time, I had been consumed with fear and uncertainty about my immediate future. I had only been arrested a few times before and had never been held more than a day. Some men may have been unconcerned about how they would manage locked away with other men, men who had, in some cases, earned the right to be feared by others both in and out of jail, but truthfully, I wasn't one of them. I was very uncertain about how I would handle myself being incarcerated over a long period of time without others I knew and trusted for support. But, from the beginning, I made a hard promise to myself that I would become whomever I needed to be to survive. I was not a victim and I wouldn't be one, even if it killed me.

When first arrested, I was unknown, skinny, and undernourished. Very few connected Jim (Mack) Evans, Black Panther cadre leader, with this thin, skinny man arrested under the alias of Greg Winston. My wild thoughts, crazy dreams, and fear were more than enough to keep me ample company in those early days.

Now, twenty-two weeks later, I was heavier and definitely much stronger. As I described, Phillip and I had one of the most ardent training routines you can imagine, including hundreds of pushups and sit-ups each day, sparring with full contact to the body, and hundreds of repetitive hand strikes and kicks. We had no training equipment, just our bodies, the bars on our cell doors that we used for military pushups, and the concrete walls of the cell block we used to condition our hands. I can imagine it was a scary sight for the guards to see two inmates in deep horseback riding stances pounding the stone walls with punches, knife-hand, and palm strikes, every day without fail.

My muscles were bigger, my hands were calloused and deadly, and I had established a solid reputation affording me some respect. All the same, I was still facing the death penalty after my trial and sure conviction. I had no idea where I was destined to go. Would I be sent to some federal facility in another part of the country in the Midwest or East Coast where I was completely unknown? Would I ever see my family again? Would I die in prison?

These questions plagued me, and without distraction, I knew they could begin to affect my emotional stability. So, picking a good book from my friend's cart was a lot more involved than it might seem, though my choices were slim to say the least: a cowboy book by Louis L'Amour or a book on meditation. I had read L'Amour previously and enjoyed his stories, but something stopped me from picking up his book. This time I wanted something more substantial. I wanted to start improving myself. Just because I was locked in a dark hole and might never get out did not mean I couldn't still learn new things and improve my mind. I remembered this was something George Jackson constantly preached. Your body can be imprisoned, but your mind could be as free as you trained it to be. With this in mind, the only other option was the meditation book. I don't remember the author or title, but I do remember what happened next.

As I began to read and practice the meditative techniques in the book, I was reminded of how it felt to pray. Though I had never stopped believing in God, I hadn't prayed in years, and I had absolutely no relationship with Him. That was about to change.

I want to pause here to make it perfectly clear that I am not advocating or championing New Age practices or theology. If God wants to reach you, He can and will use anything He pleases to do so, just like when He used the mouth of a donkey to rebuke Balaam (see Numbers 22:22-31).

Over the next couple of days, as I meditated, I began to feel a peace I had not felt in years, if ever. With practice, I began to go deeper and deeper into myself. It felt as if I could leave my circumstances behind and go wherever I wanted. While meditating, I had no concerns or worries; everything seemed to lift off of me. I held onto that book and wouldn't trade it in for another. My trustee-librarian friend didn't press me to return it, and I'm sure it wasn't in high demand.

After a couple of days, when I was particularly deep in meditation, I heard a voice. It is hard to describe the nature of this voice. It could have been external, but I knew it wasn't. I knew it was a personal experience, and I knew no one could hear it even if there had been someone present. I also knew that, even though it seemed to be coming from deep inside me, it wasn't me either. I definitely was not the source.

It was as though I had gone somewhere deep inside myself and had met someone there. I didn't know it then, but when you become a believer and give yourself to Christ as I had done as a child, the Holy Spirit comes to dwell in you and you in Him. Today, I am convinced that was Who I met that day in a deep meditative state: the Holy Spirit.

The Voice said to me, "You're getting out!"

I was shocked to hear a distinct voice in myself but not of myself. After recovering somewhat from the initial shock, I thought, What?

The Voice repeated, "You're getting out!"

Once again I repeated "What?" and added, "What do you mean?"

"Yes, you're getting out!"

"What is this? Who is this?"

No answer.

"I'm facing the death penalty or at least life. How can I be getting out?"

The Voice answered, "You're getting out. We aren't done with you!"

That was the complete exchange. As quickly as the voice had come, it was gone. As I sat there trying to make some sense of what had just happened, a feeling of certainty came over me. Was I insane? No. Was I hallucinating or just in some way self-deluded? No. Somehow I knew the Voice I heard was real and from a divine source. There was absolutely no questioning what I had just heard and experienced. At the time, I didn't have any theological training to help me analyze this encounter, but somehow I knew I could trust that Voice. I had no natural explanation for it. It was supernatural. I was getting out of there, and it would be soon. There was absolutely no doubt in my mind, and a few days later this prophecy became a reality.

CHAPTER 12

FREEDOM

A day went by, then two, then three. I felt suspended in time, like the space travelers in suspended animation I read about in sci-fi novels, except I wasn't moving. I was waiting—waiting for the reality that was sure to come. I knew the Voice hadn't lied. I didn't feel that It could lie even if It wanted to.

After a few days, I was told my lawyer had come for a visit. As I was escorted to the conference room, anticipation grew. I felt breakthrough on the horizon like a tangible thing. Every sense was heightened as the door opened and I entered that room. There I saw Andrew and my good friend Paul, with whom I'd been arrested. Paul had his big work boots propped up on the table and was smoking one of the biggest cigars I'd ever seen stuck between a huge, very cheesy grin. Andrew was also smiling and giving me a very knowing look. My first words were, "We're getting out, aren't we?"

Andrew nodded, though he still had a very quizzical look on his face. Paul, without hesitation, rose, came towards me with his arms spread wide, and gave me a massive hug (about as massive as his 5' 6" frame could muster). Paul may not have been a big man, but he was big in heart and personality. I loved him.

After accepting a cigar from Andrew, I asked, "How? How is this possible?"

All Andrew knew was the federal prosecutor informed his office that they were declining to prosecute at this time, but that since we had been arraigned they could, by law, re-arrest us and bring us back to court whenever they chose. It was speculated that perhaps the Fed's witnesses had refused to cooperate or that they did not want to expose any informants or undercover operatives they had in place at the time.

I didn't tell anyone about the Voice. I didn't know how to. How does one explain something like that? I knew they had no grid for such an experience either, so I kept it to myself but could not stop thinking about it. As we talked, I knew something or Someone had orchestrated this sudden turn of events for some reason, but explain it? I could not.

We were soon released from federal custody, and I said goodbye to San Francisco County Jail, 7th Floor Bryant Street, Federal Holding Facility for the last time with no regrets. I would always wonder what would happen to Blink, Al, and Phillip. I knew I would never visit them, even if the authorities allowed it. I would never want them exposed to whatever the future held for me on the outside. I knew they would have plenty to deal with on the inside without my bringing extra heat on them. Right now, they were just some guys who had been held on the same tier as me for the last several months (months that seemed like years, but months all the same).

I had no idea what the government, and especially the FBI, had in store for Black Panther and Black Liberation Army suspected operatives. I knew that several of these folks had been found dead, execution-style, in the past two years. There were no more raids of Panther houses or BLA suspected centers, just people disappearing without a trace or the occasional execution-style slaying. Whether you agreed with their methods or not, young people were dying for their beliefs. These were tragic and painful times.

ALAMEDA COUNTY JAIL, SANTA RITA

Paul and I were released from Federal custody, but we did not see the streets just yet. We were both transferred into the custody of the State of California and deposited across the Bay at Alameda County Jail, Santa Rita.

Wendell was not transported with us. Years later, when I connected again with Phillip through social media, having stumbled upon his profile in a very bizarre fashion, I found out that Wendell had done some serious time in state prison. He was not originally one of our group, but he and a few others from his group had been in the same house with us when we were arrested.

Paul and I were housed in a division of Santa Rita containing a large complex made up of five large dormitories. My dorm, which housed forty to fifty men on bunkbeds, formed the top of the horseshoe-shaped configuration, with two dorms each forming the arms of the horseshoe. Each dorm had a walkway in front of it running its length. These walks were encaged so prisoners could not have physical contact with prisoners in an adjacent dorm. Once per day for an hour, the guards would open the gates separating the dorms so that prisoners could move about freely amongst the five dormitories. They were also opened during mealtime to allow prisoners to report to the mess hall. These were good times to catch up with friends, but some used them to seek revenge on enemies or worse.

I was in Santa Rita less than a week before a Superior Court judge dismissed all the state charges. I connected with Paul as much as

I could during that time, just to catch up and check on him. He was his usual self, smiling and self-confident like he didn't have a care in the world.

If I thought life in the Bryant Street facility was tough, it didn't hold a candle to Santa Rita. As I said earlier, each dorm held forty to fifty men (maybe more). Many of them knew each other from the streets or from earlier incarcerations. Paul was my only acquaintance, and he was housed in another dorm. When the doors of the dormitory were locked after dinner, we were on our own. I went from a situation where I had friends and some credentials to a place where the mentalities were the same, but no one knew me, not even my Panther connections. It had been months since my picture had been in the newspaper and there were no Panthers present.

But, I still had the Voice and the promise. I knew the promise of release wasn't just out of federal custody, but a promise of total freedom. This certainty sustained me and gave me strength and a sort of courageous confidence that I'm sure the other prisoners could sense. I was being checked out, assessed, and profiled; I could feel the eyes and the stares. This confidence, and the hundred pushups I did on my knuckles on the concrete floor every morning and night, I'm sure helped forestall any attempts to "try" the new guy, at least until I was released.

Then, one morning, I got the summons to appear in court. I was transported to the Alameda County Courthouse in downtown Oakland that morning. I don't remember a whole lot about that day, but I do remember it was sunny for a fall day. When it was my turn, I was ushered in before the judge whose name I have long forgotten. I do remember, however, having the feeling that something good was about to happen. The judge was silent for a moment. There was no defense attorney or prosecutor present, just me, his honor, a bailiff, and a guard from the jail.

He looked up from the court documents he was reading, gave me a long look, and finally spoke. He wanted me to explain in my own words the charges before me. I felt an initial check. I had been indoctrinated to say nothing before law enforcement or a judge without a lawyer present, but I remembered the Voice. I was sure this whole thing was being orchestrated, so I spoke. About two sentences into my narrative, the judge stated he was not interested in my past activities, affiliations, or political views. He just wanted to know what had taken place during those three days of occupation of Merritt College leading to these California state charges.

I explained the events of the three days, starting with our entry to the executive offices and the college president's willing departure from his office into the hallway, though I did escort him into the hands of colleagues who then escorted him to the street. Our occupation of the buildings was in peaceful protest without harm to anyone, until the police came in and the physical struggle that resulted as the protestors resisted. I admitted that, as the protest leader, I did ignore the authorities' orders to vacate the premises. I shocked myself with the candor I exhibited, but somehow knew it was the right thing to do at this very pivotal point in my life. I knew because of the Voice.

When I was done, the judge laughingly asked me how long I'd been in custody. I answered several months. When I saw him shake his balding head back and forth in a slow pensive motion, laughing as he looked over the papers before him, I knew something life-altering was about to happen. I had never seen a judge of any kind, let alone a Superior Court judge, laugh in open court before. After a few forever-long seconds, he looked up at me.

"Mr. Evans, if you plead guilty to misdemeanor disturbing the peace, which is the lowest charge on the books, I will dismiss these other charges and I will give you credit for time served. Will you plead guilty to this charge?"

I was in shock. I had expected something miraculous, but not this. This meant my immediate release. Though I'd have to go back to Santa Rita for processing, most likely I would probably be out of custody within twenty-four hours. Though in shock, my mind registered all of this very quickly, and the thought occurred to me that I had better respond before he changed his mind. I blurted out, "Guilty!" He laughed again, but I couldn't care less. The man could have undressed and danced in his underwear for all I cared. I had been facing death and now, in a few hours, I would be totally free. No probation, no parole. A total miracle.

I was transported back to Santa Rita and released early the next day. I had no money and was wearing my only possessions, a pair of jeans, boots, and a T-shirt that by now was two sizes too small. No one knew I was getting out. I had no ride and was penniless. I walked through the gates of Santa Rita straight to the nearest road and started hitchhiking. Two young girls, who I guess thought it was daring and adventurous to pick up a stranger near the county prison, picked me up. The next thing I knew, I was on the 580 freeway speeding toward Oakland.

As the girls made nervous small talk, I realized I had no idea where I was going. None of my friends had visited or made any contact with any of us while in jail, and had been wise to not do so. Visiting us, as hot as we were, would have only brought our friends' unwanted attention and scrutiny. I didn't know what I was going to do or where I was going to go. I really hadn't thought that far ahead. It was very surreal. After several months, I was free. Now what?

I hadn't been in the East Bay in some time, and my friends weren't exactly known for keeping the same address for very long. I also knew that these young white girls were having their little adventure but would never in a million years take me home to Mommy and Daddy. I still had an out-of-control Afro and was very obviously an outlaw. The full extent of their little foray into the dark side was to get me where I was going and no further. I soon rescued them from their growing anxiety by asking them to pull their car over at the Ashby Street exit on the 101 freeway in Berkeley. From there, I disappeared into the familiar streets of Berkeley and Oakland.

me, ver. 26.
things, ch. 15. 26.
Ac. 2. 33.
es to your i Or, several
whatsoever I from me.
said unto you. ch. 2. 22
& 12. 16
47 'Peace I leave with you, & 16. 13.
1 Jn. 2. 20.
"my peace I give unto you: 27.
not as the world giveth, gi
unto you. Let not yo
be troubled

u, and
bringeth
'withou'
6 If a n
is cast
is wit
them
fire

another
may abide

Spiri

CHAPTER 13

FREE BUT LOST

As the days went by, I tracked down a friend here and there, but most of them were strangely standoffish. I later found out that many of them thought the only way I could have gotten out of the situation I had been in was to have informed on someone. The thought didn't occur to them that I very well may have been in jail because someone had informed on me, and that I was out because: 1) they would not testify, 2) the government didn't want to blow their cover yet and was still using them, or 3) they had no case against me in the first place. They also hadn't noticed that no one had been arrested while I was in jail or since my release.

Huey Newton sent word to me that I had his permission to stay in the Bay Area as long as I didn't engage in any "movement" activities and stayed away from any Panther locations or people. I laughed, as I had no intention of having anything to do with the Party. I just wanted to heal and explore the supernatural. That Voice had been real. Something much bigger than the Black Panther Party, Huey P. Newton, Bobby Seal, and the life I had been leading was out there waiting for me to discover it. Though I didn't know it then, there is a proverb that states, "It is the honor of God to conceal a thing, but the honor of Kings to search out a matter" (Proverbs 25:2 *One New Man Bible*).

It was a very long time before I shared my transcendental experience with anyone. Who would I tell, and who would believe it? I kept it to myself and began the process of getting free of all the baggage, disappointment, frustration, fear, and anger I'd accumulated since leaving my family church as a youngster.

As time passed, I began to transition out of the soldier mentality that kept me hyper-vigilant twenty-four-seven. The expectation of big-booted police officers with handcuffs and warrants in their hands kicking in my front door at any time to re-arrest me began to fade over the next few years as I started rebuilding my life. Though I had had a supernatural experience with something or Someone that I didn't understand, I still was not a candidate for citizen of the year. While working part-time at various jobs, I still roamed the streets and soon found that money came along much easier with an illegal hustle than working minimum wage. I became involved in activities such as moving illegal merchandise and selling small quantities of weed. Finding contacts to fuel these enterprises was not difficult; those were plentiful.

Before I was arrested, a Black Panther Party officer by the name of Doug Miranda had approached me with a proposition. Doug said the Party had been monitoring our work through the Merritt College Black Student Union and was interested in working with us. Furthermore, since I had worked with the Party in the past, I was already considered an associate. This was news to me because I didn't think they even knew I existed. For months, I had shown up every day and sold as many papers as I could while waiting to be given something more substantial to do. I soon got tired of waiting, enrolled in Merritt College and eventually revived the BSU.

Doug went on to say that not only did the Party want to work with us, but they would also roll any member of the BSU who wanted it into the Party as members. After a vote and a show of hands, we agreed and became Panthers. Our assignment was to work on college and high school campuses, speaking wherever we were invited with no strings attached from Panther higher-ups. It worked well, and soon we were given a building in North Berkeley that had been a Panther school and now became North Berkeley Black Panther Headquarters. This building also housed the National Committee to Combat Fascism (NCCF), the organization whose membership included a young woman who was destined to be my wife.

I first came across Paula while I was still running the Black Student Union at Merritt College and doing campus education for the Panthers (before moving to the building we were later given). She was attending an alternative high school in the East Bay, and they invited a Party representative—me—to speak to their eleventh-grade class. I gave my speech to the class and left without meeting her. Much later, after meeting at the home of mutual friends, she reminded me of the occasion.

Paula was still young, but there was something about her innocence, purity, courage, and zeal for life that just made everyone fall in love with her. Of course, her beauty didn't hurt either! Though I was attracted to her, I struggled. She was white. I had briefly dated a white woman back in DC, and it didn't end well. We were okay with one another but just different. It was like we didn't speak the same language. Our cultural norms were out of sync, and it just didn't work.

Paula, however, had been a member of a group that was sanctioned by the Panthers and had done many joint ventures together. She, I later discovered, had stood on the front lines with us, and a photograph of her attending George Jackson's funeral had even been published in a pictorial book about the Panthers. Furthermore, unbeknownst to me, she was often at the NCCF headquarters located on the ground floor of the two-story Panther chapter I oversaw in Berkeley.

We actually had an amazing amount in common, got along well, and spoke the same language, but she was white and I was black! I wasn't sure I wanted to take on that struggle in 1972 America. Our friends in common were an interracial couple. My old friend Joe Stephens and Paula's good friend Gail from the NCCF were a couple and making it work, but very few people in those days were successful in making an interracial relationship work. The racism and the pressures were enormous.

As I debated my uncertainty, I sensed that Voice again. It was not as strong and definitive as before, but the message was, Suppose this is the woman I have ordained for you? Will you let something as immaterial as skin color keep you from her?

I took Paula on our first date two months before her nineteenth birthday. This was twice now the Voice had spoken to me. It had proven to be accurate and trustworthy. You would think by now I would have learned. One thing is for certain, the best decision I ever made, other than giving my life to my Lord Jesus Christ, was to follow that Voice regarding Paula. I will talk more about her later, but that first date was the beginning of a powerful relationship that has lasted forty-six years and continues to go strong. Our life has seen its ups and downs and bumps in the road, but it has been blessed beyond measure. It has been full of love and has produced tremendous fruit that was unimaginable for us in those days.

When I was a young boy, I practically lived in our Baptist church on 13th Street in northwest Washington, DC. I believed there was a God and believed all the biblical stories. I was baptized when I was very young because I wanted to be baptized. It was my decision, no one forced me, and no one tried to talk me into it. I felt the need to do it, so I asked, my parents agreed, and it was done. I was probably six years old. I poured my heart into learning more about God and serving in the church. I gobbled up honors and titles: president of the Sunday school class, head junior usher, most decorated Boy Scout in our church chapter's history, and so on. We children were taught all about the heroes of the Bible and their exploits, but I was curious. I wanted to know more. I wanted to understand who God was. What was God's nature? How did He function and operate in my everyday life? Why did so many of my prayers go unanswered? I tried reading my old King James Bible but never got very far. I was never taught how to read the Bible and didn't even know the difference between the New Testament and the Old. I just started reading at Genesis and fell asleep by the tenth page every night because I didn't understand a word of it.

I wrote about my church experiences and the subsequent disillusionment that followed earlier, so I will not go into more detail here. The point I'm making is I knew about God and I tried to pursue Him in the only way I knew, but I didn't know God in any real sense or in a personal way. I certainly had never heard His voice, so when I did hear the Voice I was confused by it. Was it some disembodied spirit communicating with me? Was it some close relative that had passed on before me? Was it God? Was it the devil? I didn't know, but I wanted to.

...me, xc. 24. 49. and
ver. 16. bringeth
things, ch. 15. 26. without
As. 2. 33. 6 If a n
s to your i Or. is cast
whatsoever I severed is wit
from me. them.
said unto you. i ch. 2. 22 fire.
27 'Peace I leave with you, & 12. 16
"my peace I give unto you; & 16. 13.
not as the world giveth, g i Jn. 2. 20,
unto you. Let not yo a Mt. 11.
be troubled
another
may abide
or;
the Spirit

CHAPTER 14

DAZED AND CONFUSED

Over the next few years, I became more and more fascinated by the supernatural while continuing to make my living in one illegal hustle after another. I was living in darkness while simultaneously pursuing the supernatural. This will sound schizophrenic to most of you, but to some this will sound very familiar.

Before too long, the quest to know and experience more in the realm of the supernatural overcame my drive to continue to make money through illegal means. I began to experiment in visualization, deep meditation, astral projection, and other New Age stuff. I had long sessions with the Ouija board, contacting all sorts of spiritual beings, most pretending to be friendly. My wife and I sensed danger in that activity and soon cut it off. We read all sorts of metaphysical writings from *The Teachings of Don Juan by Carlos Castaneda* to the *Seth Speaks* series by Jane Roberts to *A Course in Miracles* by Helen Schucman and William Thetford. We had some fantastical experiences, even experiencing a brief astral projection where I left my body, turned over, saw myself lying there (I looked dead), panicked, and returned in a flash. I never repeated that exercise again.

My wife, my friend André, and I wanted to move out of Oakland. We did not intend to give up our lucrative marijuana business at this time, but felt that we had outgrown the Bay Area. We talked and decided what our new property was to look like, including a separate granny flat or guest house on the property for André, three separate backyards for our pit bulls, a four-bedroom layout and design, and in a specific neighborhood in Santa Rosa, California that we liked. We made a detailed drawing of the house and property, studied it, committed the drawing to memory, and visualized it together while holding hands. The next day André and I drove from Oakland to Santa Rosa and plopped the drawing down on a real estate agent's desk. She recognized the place immediately and took us there in five minutes. The place was available, affordable, and vacant. We produced first and last month's rent and were living on the property by the month's end. It was totally, off the charts, weird.

Let's be clear again here—I am, in no way, promoting New Age philosophy, spiritualism, or any other dark practices. This was simply the journey of three poorly prepared young people trying to understand the things of the physical world and the spiritual without proper guidance or mentorship. Though we were dazed and confused, out of this experience and others we learned that 1) the spirit realm is real, and 2) man truly does have dominion. What we did not know was that a living God created these physical and spiritual principles, and that there is an enemy of man that will guide you into misuse of these principles if you do not have the Holy Spirit of God to guide you. We were being mentored, but by unseen forces we didn't understand.

We lived in Santa Rosa and then Cotati, California for years. André eventually got married and went his own way. Paula and I had two boys in the County of Sonoma. Joaquin was born in Santa Rosa, and Jahi was born in Cotati. We were as happy as two people could be with me living a duplicitous life as a college student/athlete and the neighborhood drug dealer.

I was a very good student. It was amazing I was able to keep a 3.5 GPA while dealing and using my own product as well as playing basketball on the university's club team. It was a recipe for disaster, and I soon hit rock bottom.

LIVING TOO FAST

I graduated from college the year my second son was born and was accepted into a private graduate studies program in Marin County. It was a yearlong course of study, and once again I was able to fool everyone, including myself, and complete the program. Now, I was certified in clinical modalities for the treatment of psychosomatic illnesses (biofeedback, for short).

Next, I was accepted into a master's program in psychology and began my studies the following fall. Along the way, the pressures of the double life I was leading began to mount, and as time went by, I used more cocaine. I began to freebase it—a process whereby one turns the cocaine powder or flake into a small dry rock, which sometime later became known as rock cocaine. Over time, my use got out of hand, and it affected my performance in the classroom, on the basketball court, and at my job.

I was awarded a much sought-after grant for psych students to work in a state-funded psychiatric facility, a job I took great pride in. My formal job was to assist the recreational therapist with developmentally disabled adult men in a locked unit on the grounds of this huge state-run facility. That was my job description, but my real job was to do whatever I was told, and to fill in when and where needed.

I took the job seriously. I wanted to learn and to serve the staff and residents of the program to the best of my ability. I found them all to be fascinating people. The staff came from every background imaginable. Most of the men and women were truly good people and wanted to make life better for those in their care. It was interesting how many had become psychiatric technicians, nurses, or orderlies. Some became psych-techs because it was a shorter training program than becoming a licensed vocational nurse (LVN). Some became LVNs because it was a shorter program than becoming a registered nurse (RN). Some RNs were there because local hospitals and other medical establishments weren't hiring at the time. No matter the reason, most were building a résumé to land a job somewhere else, and some were doing exactly what they wanted to do. Those folks were the "lifers." Some lifers were looking forward to retirement and their government pensions, and some had little ambition or hope of doing anything else. They had families and simply needed the job and the paycheck. Regardless of the reason, most were trying to make a difference while they were there.

I felt very fortunate to be a graduate student assistant, a job dozens of other grad students coveted, but that feeling only lasted a few weeks until the unit supervisor finally told me what separated me from the other applicants with similar GPAs—I had a black belt in martial arts. What? I was pretty upset. There I was thinking I had some academic attribute that stood out from the rest of the psychology grad students competing for this job, when really they needed someone who could handle themselves and wasn't afraid of the very violent population we were tasked with supervising. It was a small letdown, but I was still glad to get the job. As a grad student, the job counted toward credits for graduation with my master's degree. It was work that gave me real-life experience in the field, and it paid pretty well.

The most violent men in this state-run hospital were separated into two units: small-to-medium-sized men in one unit and large men (over two hundred pounds) in the other. I was assigned to the former. The building they lived in was a large building capable of housing a hundred-plus men separated into three living dorms, staff office and business spaces, and a backyard for recreational activities and exercise. The men who were "higher functioning" were allowed to go out on the general hospital grounds on supervised outings.

It only took a few days for me to see why they wanted someone who could handle himself in a physical confrontation. Part of my job as an assistant to the recreational director was to make sure the guys who were capable got plenty of exercise. This included going outside the building and, on occasion, walking the grounds of the hospital. On an outing with the recreational director and seven or eight of our residents, a resident became agitated, and the RD had to take him back to the unit. To my surprise, she instructed me to continue the outing with the rest of the group—my first time alone with a group. I felt a bit of anxiety, but I had learned years ago to face challenges and my fears, so off we went.

I began a conversation with one of the young men, let's call him George. This young man was a savant. He was an avid daily reader of the *San Francisco Times* and could tell you the day of the week for any date you gave him, no matter how far you went in the past or into the future. George's gift was tested frequently, and he never failed. When a staff member asked (trying to trip him up or because he just didn't know the answer), "George! What day of the week would February 29, 2019, fall on?" George would answer with absolutely no facial affect. "There wouldn't be a day. February 29, 2019 will not exist. March 1, 2019, will be on a Friday."

However, George was also quite violent. On this particular day, we were walking and talking when suddenly George leapt for my throat. He had wrapped his fingers around my neck before it had even registered to me that he had moved. He was amazingly strong, but I managed to leverage him with a hip roll and take him softly to the ground with a controlled roll, which broke his grip. I was shaken and slightly panicked. What would I do if the other residents started to freak out at the sight of violence? I had seen this happen on the unit. When a resident became violent, others reacted by going into an uncontrollable frenzy themselves. I was by myself with too many men, a program violation, and was still in training. It was no one's fault—we were always in a shortage crisis in terms of personnel. Always.

Thankfully, George calmed almost immediately and resumed his normal, friendly demeanor as if nothing had happened. As for me, no one had prepared me for this—not my professors at the university, nor my supervisors and co-workers on the unit. I felt I had just dodged a major bullet. I wasn't quite sure what had just happened, but I released the biggest sigh of relief when I finally got everyone back to the unit without a scratch.

When I reported the incident to my superiors, all I got back was blank looks. To them, these incidents were commonplace and to be expected. They just assumed I was aware and prepared to deal with it. The unit supervisor, however, was not happy. He thought I had shown aptitude for the work, but was disappointed to hear that at this point in my training I had been out with a group alone. I was just glad to have gotten everyone back in one piece.

I learned two things that day:

1) The people I was tasked to work with could and would become violent for no apparent reason and exhibit no build-up to it.

2) This was not school. This was the real world of working in the field of mental health.

Meanwhile, I continued to abuse cocaine and spiral downward into a very dark and dangerous place. My drug deals grew more intense as I became connected to and did business with some very hardcore people in the Oakland-Berkeley area. I don't wish to delve further into this chapter of my life because I have no desire to glorify the lifestyle of being a drug dealer. I only mention it to illustrate how far one can fall and how deep our Lord and Savior can reach into the depths of hell to redeem those He died for, as many times as is necessary.

CHAPTER 15

ROCK BOTTOM

I had been up all evening, well past midnight, partying and doing coke all by myself. Paula and the kids were asleep in their beds when I received a desperate call from the hospital. They had a number of staff calling in sick and were in dire need of help. Though I was in no shape to drive, I agreed to come in. It wasn't the smartest decision I'd ever made in my life. As a matter of fact, it was quite dumb.

Drugs, especially drugs like cocaine, can make one feel invincible. The drug lies and tells you that you are the smartest, cleverest, most ingenious individual in the world. It would have you believe you can drive the fastest of vehicles on the most treacherous of back roads, making hairpin turns one after another as fast as that vehicle could go.

This is the lie it was telling me on that night on that road. I had my red MG wide open, careening around curve after curve, laughing my head off, knowing with cocaine-fueled confidence I was the best driver in the world.

Suddenly, my rear tires failed to grab hold of the road as I negotiated one particularly nasty curve, and I spun out of control. I had zero command over the MG as it spun and spun in what seemed like a hundred rotations. It's funny how fast you can sober up when your life is hanging by a thread. Before I knew it, I saw an old broken-down, chicken-wire fence speeding toward me. I have no idea how fast I was going when I hit that fence. All I know is I witnessed another miracle. Somehow that rickety old fence held and stopped my speeding car dead in its tracks. Thank God I had my seatbelt on (one smart thing I did that night).

I sat there in a daze, thinking this old fence must be sturdier than it looked. I got out of the car and walked around to the fence. My right headlamp was snagged in the chicken wire and my front bumper had hit a worn, weather-beaten, wooden fence post. There was no way that old fence should have stopped my car, and yet it did. I looked over the fence and saw a ten-to-twelve-foot gully on the other side with a very small stream running through it. If I had gone through that fence and had been knocked unconscious, there was no telling how long I would have lain there exposed to cold and dampness. It was not out of the realm of possibility that I could have died that night.

We aren't done with you!

If that weren't enough of a miracle, my car actually started right up. I sat there for a long while, trying to take it all in. I wasn't ready to accept the inevitable yet. I was still resisting the call on my life, but I knew the hand of Providence had interceded on my behalf that night once again.

After a few minutes, I got my car back on the road and drove very carefully to the hospital. I wasn't going to tempt another accident. I was too grateful to be alive.

However, the night still held a little more excitement. I was assigned to a unit that was short of any supervision. The residents were tucked away, supposedly asleep in their cots. There was a young man in this particular unit's dorm who, by reputation, was extremely dangerous. He liked to play with his own feces. (I know this is a very gross part of my story, but it is quite true. Some of God's creatures have an extremely poor lot in life. It's not God's fault, but rather the fault of this fallen world. That's a subject I cover in another book I've written entitled *What DOES God Do All Day?!*). Anyway, this poor soul was a carrier of several diseases. I don't remember them all, but I do remember he had some form of hepatitis. We as a staff were repeatedly warned to avoid being scratched by this man. He would not allow anyone to cut his fingernails, so they were extremely long. Due to his fascination with his own feces, his fingernails were always filthy.

By the time I started work I was pretty sober, but I can't say I wasn't still a tad bit under the influence. I entered the dorm, closed the door behind me, and waited for my eyes to adjust to the dark. The room wasn't completely dark, as windows high on the walls allowed moonlight to filter through. Faint light from the common room and nearby staff areas also passed in through a couple windows in and around the door. Even so, it was dark enough I was blind for a few seconds as I adjusted to the dim light. The place smelled of feces and disinfectant. The stench was alive.

Everything seemed to be under control. The staff nurse who was trying to cover the dorm and her other responsibilities was very glad to see me. She rushed away with a quick "thank you" for coming in. Before leaving, the nightshift supervisor once again warned me to be vigilant. "Stay awake!"

I found an empty bench and took a seat. I was glad to find one, because for some reason, many of the guys preferred to sleep on the benches rather than their cots. Perhaps the option to choose a bench over a cot gave them the illusion they had some modicum of control over their lives and environment. It was a meager concession by the staff. Only the strongest and most feared could control their own bench, creating a hierarchy of sorts.

Except for an occasional rustling sound and a lot of snoring, the room seemed to be as it should. I sat for a time, then got up and walked around, inspecting the guys as they slept. I soon found the young man I mentioned earlier sleeping on a bench right across from where my bench was located.

I repeated my up and down inspection routine for a while, but was desperately fighting sleep. I couldn't concentrate, and despite my best efforts, I found myself starting to drift off. I don't even remember sliding to a prone position on my right side on the bench and don't know how long I was lying there, probably no more than a minute or two, when something tugged me back to a semi-conscious state —just in time to a see a dark creature slowly lurking before me. Just as suddenly, it leapt toward me. It was the young man I most feared. Time came to a standstill. He was now airborne, hands spread like eagle's talons. I had no time to think. Instinctively, I struck out with a left-legged sidekick while still lying on my right side. The kick caught him square in the chest. This young man probably weighed all of a hundred-and-five pounds, if that. The kick caught him perfectly and propelled him backward, where he hit the ground and slid back under the bench he'd been sleeping on.

I immediately sat up and looked around to see if any staff person had entered the dorm or if any of the residents had been awakened by the noise, though there had been none except for the sound of the sudden exhalation of breath as my foot made contact with his torso. Everything seemed to be normal except for my heart pounding a hole in my chest and a man quivering under a bench. The whole thing would have been funny, like a cartoon, if it had not been so terrifying. It was like a scene out of a comedic horror movie.

Needless to say, I didn't come close to sleeping after that, and my friend remained under his bench until the day shift relief came on duty. It was an unbelievable night, and I can't blame you if you doubt its veracity, but I vouch that every word is true and accurate.

BROTHERLY LOVE

I didn't learn from my jailhouse visitation, and I didn't learn from almost killing myself on that dark back road. I continued down a dark tunnel to hell, full speed ahead.

Soon, I was let go at the hospital. They claimed the grant money had run out. While I didn't know if that was true or not, I suspected that as medical professionals they were aware of the signs and symptoms of my substance abuse.

Meanwhile, my wife's family graciously had allowed us to purchase her grandfather's house in Arcata, California for half of what it was worth and no money down. We could not have afforded our first home without this great gift. One day, in the middle of the move to Arcata, Paula announced she'd had enough. She said she was taking the kids to the new house, and I was not to follow until I decided what was most important in my life: my family or cocaine. She is a strong woman and means what she says. She kept her word and left.

I stayed in our house, which was now all but empty—just a mattress in the master bedroom, a chair or two in the living room, and my bench and weights. That big empty house felt like a snow cave in the Himalayas. I'd never felt so alone seeing only grey. While in the deepest of pits, suicide crossed my mind.

I knew I was at a crossroads. I had a major decision to make, one that would determine the rest of my life. But God is good. He illustrated the two roads for me, clear as a living roadmap. One road led to sure death, a death that would occur in approximately six months by overdose or being murdered during a drug deal gone bad, as had happened to others I knew. The other road led to reuniting with my family, seeing my kids grow up, and happiness. It was real, and I knew beyond a shadow it was real.

As I sat there contemplating these roads, there came a very loud, aggressive knock on the door, jolting me out of my daydream. It was the kind of aggressive knock the police make that says, "Open up! We know you're in there!" I went to the door fully expecting to see an army of grim-faced cops ready for combat, but to my surprise, it was four of the psych techs I'd worked with at the hospital.

All I could do was stand there, staring. This was the absolute last scene I had expected to see. What were they doing here? How did they even know where I lived? I knew these guys, and I knew this wasn't a robbery or whatever, but they looked so determined and almost pissed.

I don't even remember standing aside before finding them in my living room. I tried to make feeble small talk and act like I had not been contemplating whether to kill myself. I must have been a pitiful sight, standing there in an empty house, so skinny I could barely hold my pants up, trying to pretend I had just been elected king of the world. Their faces communicated loud and clear they were having none of it. There was no point in playing games. They were here to confront me and confront me they did.

I don't know if any of you have ever had the pleasure of being surrounded by a handful of veteran, hard-nosed, psychiatric technicians or not, but trust me, it's unnerving. Even with all I had been through in my thirty years, when they began to speak, I sat down, shut up, and listened.

I felt hot pokers of shame piercing deep into my spirit as they spoke. They spoke life into me. They told me I was bright, strong, and worthy. They told me I had an amazing future ahead of me, and they talked about how much it pained them to see me throwing my future away. They told me I wasn't fooling them one bit and challenged me to pull my head out of my rear end. They talked about my former co-workers and how positively they saw me. Rivers of guilt flowed through me as they confessed most of them had "maxed out" in life and gone about as far as their educations, skills, and ambitions could take them. In me, they saw someone who had wonders ahead of him and could have just about anything he wanted out of life.

Then, as suddenly as they had come, they left. I never saw them again. I don't know how long I sat there, but I knew what I had experienced was a miracle of brotherly love. These men somehow wrangled my address from human resources and drove miles from their homes in neighboring towns on their day off to pour into a young black man on the verge of a decision leading to life or death—a man they would probably never see again (unless it was at his funeral). I will never forget them and the brotherly love that crossed all racial barriers they demonstrated that day. God had intervened once again. How else could I explain it? What could motivate these very busy men, most of them with families and highly stressful jobs, to go out of their way like this? In retrospect, I see God's hand all over this. My son, Joaquin, believes they may have been angels. He just may be right. I'll find out in heaven.

Their visit was the confirmation I needed. I called my wife and told her I was choosing my family. I gathered a few things, got in the car still reeling from the drugs in my system, and drove from the Northern Bay Area of Sonoma County to Humboldt County, California. I was in no condition to drive, but I knew if I didn't take action right then I might never have the strength to do it.

In my intoxicated state, I talked to my friend André all the way up highway 101 and reached Arcata before dark, which was impossible. It was a four-hour plus drive and should have been well past dark by the time I arrived. I know I was under the influence and had no business driving, but my friend kept me focused the whole way, warning me to stay alert and watch the traffic as I drove. The only problem was that Dré wasn't with me. I had actually driven the entire trip by myself. I can only conclude I was completely hallucinating, or God sent me an angel. One could argue that my vision was the result of the drugs I had taken, but this type of hallucination had never happened before and has never occurred since. I believe God divinely intervened in my life again. Not only did my angel get me there safely, and in half the time but, miraculously, I was stone cold sober when I hugged my wife and kids in the driveway. I have not touched a cocaine pipe since.

You'd think I'd be ready to surrender to God by this point. So many things had happened that pointed me towards Him—I've only written about a few. But no, I wasn't ready yet. I was willing to concede there was a spiritual world outside this reality. I had to admit at least to that, but surrendering to an all-knowing, omnipresent God? I just wasn't ready to take that step. For a man like me, surrender was not an easy step to take. I'd spent my teenage and adult years transforming my mind and body into a tough version of my former self. I wanted no part of that underweight, sheltered, often fearful kid I had been. All my martial arts training, running, lifting, and sports were for one purpose: to turn myself into an individual hard to defeat and not very likely to yield to threats or intimidation.

But, of course, God still wasn't done with me. Once again, He tapped me on the shoulder.

CHAPTER 16

IN COMES JESUS!

Paula had studied midwifery in Sonoma County, and her training under a highly esteemed lay midwife was extremely impressive. Her coursework, reading assignments, and practical training rivaled mine as a graduate student. She graduated and became a practicing midwife before our move to Humboldt County, where she began to work with a master midwife named Jan.

Jan was very well known. Being a midwife in those days brought you into contact with a lot of New Agers. New Agers are highly spiritual folks who believe in a spirit realm and a sort of God entity that is in "all things," but also don't really believe Jesus Christ is the one true way to Father God. They are usually very well-meaning, peaceful people who experience the miraculous on occasion but are fundamentally deceived regarding the reality of the Triune God.

Jan had an acquaintance known to be a very skillful psychic. People raved about her accuracy and her ability to know things about you there was no way she could know. I had dabbled in New Age for years, and I thought if this woman was truly that gifted maybe she could help me find some answers I had been seeking forever. For example, I wanted to know if I had experienced any past lives or had a spirit guide.

I called to make an appointment. Evidently, I knew the right names to drop and was granted a session; however, there was one problem. The woman I wanted to see was not available and wouldn't be for some time. I didn't want to wait, so I accepted the invitation to meet with one of the head psychic's apprentices.

I walked into the appointed place at the appointed time and was greeted by a very pleasant, attractive young woman, who made me feel quite comfortable. After explaining the process, she began the session. She closed her eyes, got very quiet, and began to speak. She talked about past lives I was supposed to have had, and how my friends and I had been together for many lifetimes. Then she suddenly stopped. She remained dead silent, her face reflecting some inner turmoil, for several seconds until I became concerned. Finally, I asked, "Are you alright?"

Her eyes flew open. "I've never seen anything like this before!"

"Like what?"

She said, "Your spirit guide is Jesus Christ!"

We both sat there, stunned. I don't even remember leaving. I don't know if I thanked her, said goodbye, or even paid her. I'm sure I did, but that revelation was overwhelming. I had expected my spirit guide (if I had one) to be some ethereal New Age figure I had read about or who at least fit the whole past life, mystical paradigm. But Jesus? This revelation just jumped out of nowhere, a spiritual, supernatural intrusion from heaven.

What was going on? What was I to make of all these encounters I'd been experiencing the past few years? Was I supposed to start going back to church? Ugh!

In hindsight it seems so obvious to me now. Duh! Once again, in His grace, patience, and kindness, God was tapping me on the shoulder. He was calling me, and pretty soon He was going to stop tapping and start hammering.

Things went along well for a few years. Paula got a job working in the Arcata Children's Center directed by Kate Green. She started off as an administrative assistant, but due to her considerable intelligence and work ethic, soon rose to the position of assistant director. I, meanwhile, finished my thesis work for my master's in psychology while taking care of Joaquin and Jahi during the day. After earning my degree, I went to work. My first job was as a part-time instructor at Humboldt State University as an African American history professor (my minor as an undergrad). I also began work as a full-time counselor in a long-term psychiatric hospital.

Meanwhile, I had regular nightmares that I was back in my old stomping grounds destroying myself again, succumbing to the temptation to "hit the pipe." Sometimes in these dreams, I'd try to resist, but would eventually give in. In other dreams, I'd eagerly go for the pipe at a friend's offering or because I had the urge. I'd wake up in a cold sweat, heart pounding like I'd just beaten Secretariat in the Kentucky Derby. This almost nightly drama played out for three or four years before finally starting to subside. I didn't seek counseling. I was in mental health, and the stigma of my addiction getting back to my employers or anyone in the business was too much for me to contemplate. Plus, I was sure I could beat it on my own, so I continued to quietly wrestle with the addiction demon for years with my dear wife's support.

At last, one day about four years after moving to Arcata, I realized I was no longer having the nightmares. I was finally free! I'd have a dream every so often, but they were just dreams, not nightmares, and they were very rare.

MY KINGDOM INVITATION

After a few years, I earned a big promotion with the hospital chain I worked for. It was a great opportunity, but it required me to move to Bakersfield, California. Paula was completing nursing school and had to stay in Northern California. Transferring schools would cost her too many credits. The promotion meant driving several hours up from Bakersfield to Arcata to see the family every two to three weeks, but it was worth the investment in our careers. After her graduation, the family was reunited, and Paula and I even got a chance to work together at the Bakersfield facility.

We were doing great, advancing in our careers and enjoying life. One promotion led to another, and soon we were on the move again, this time to Ventura County, California. I got my first job as a nursing home administrator at a small convalescent hospital in Ojai, California. It was a small facility, but it was mine to run. I had the opportunity to succeed in the field where I had trained for so many years, and I was going to make sure I did.

The years went by, and the boys grew up and were destined for college. Paula and I were very successful in our jobs, and soon we were able to buy a home completely on our own, with no help from family. We were very proud of our house and accomplishments and were enjoying life. I continued my martial arts training under Master Yong Sup Shin in Camarillo and also decided that to advance my career even more, I should go back to school for my MBA. I enrolled in Pepperdine University and took all evening classes.

By the time I graduated from the MBA program, I had started a new enterprise, a home health agency called Horizon Home Health. My wife and I founded this company with a couple of friends, a medical doctor and his wife, who was also an RN. I had also opened my own martial arts studio in Ventura, and was still running the convalescent hospital in Ojai. Clearly, I was far too busy to think about God, but He was not too busy to think about me, or my family.

A few months after opening my taekwondo school, Premier Martial Arts, a young man from Colorado by the name of Eddie Tait walked into my school. He was in town visiting his father when he saw my school and decided to stop in. In a sense, he never left.

Eddie was about twenty years old, athletic, and had a natural propensity to see and execute martial arts techniques with ease. There was also an infectious exuberance about him. As time passed, Eddie advanced in my school faster than any I'd trained, with the exception of another phenom named Thu Huynh. Thu was Thai and had been raised in Asian culture. He was also tall, muscular, and athletic with uncanny power, courage, and an indomitable will. He is a master instructor (4th dan/degree) and still holds the record for fastest to black belt under my tutelage—one and a half years. Eddie holds second fastest at two years. My typical time frame for advancement to black belt is three and a half years.

My sons would probably have held records with Eddie and Thu, but they started so young they didn't qualify for years, though they were exceptionally talented and readily embraced traditional martial arts values such as discipline, honor, and respect. My oldest, Joaquin, was fighting in the black belt division and winning before he made the rank of black belt, and my youngest, Jahi, was nationally known and admired. At one point he was headed to the USA National Team, but God had other ideas.

But back to Eddie. He stayed and trained with me for years and became not only one of my main instructors but a part of the Evans family. Paula and I loved him like a son, Jahi and Joaquin considered him a brother. The boys had high school and college to contend with, but Eddie was married to the school. He lived it, breathed it, and was completely absorbed in the martial arts. Today he is a fourth dan and an outstanding instructor as well as pastor.

One day, Eddie announced he was moving from Ventura to Yuba City, California, just north of Sacramento, to start a business with his childhood best friend Glen. Just like that, he was gone. It wasn't as abrupt as it sounds, but it felt that way to us. His departure left a major hole in our family and in the school, and we grieved it probably more than he knows even to this day.

We did not know it then, but Eddie was being obedient to the call of the Holy Spirit. He and Glen never really got their business going, but as it turned out, that was not the real reason he was called to Northern California. Glen was an on-fire Christian, and soon Eddie found himself going to a dynamic church in the area named Glad Tidings, pastored by a man who would also become a good friend of our family's, Dave Bryan. With Glen and under the tutelage of Pastor Dave, Eddie grew rapidly in the Lord. He was the same man but changed. He still trained but found room to extend his boundless enthusiasm into his pursuit of more of the ways of God.

HOLY SPIRIT COME

Soon after Eddie moved to Yuba City, the boys moved to San Francisco, Joaquin to finish his BA at San Francisco State and Jahi to start at City College. Paula and I were suffering "empty nest syndrome" big time—not just at home but at Premier Martial Arts as well. These guys weren't just my sons and trusted assistants but also my best friends.

In August of 1999, Eddie invited the boys to make the forty-five-minute drive from "The City" to Yuba City and Glad Tidings to hear a missionary speak by the name of David Hogan. We had raised the boys to believe in the existence of the spirit and a supernatural universe, though not at all in the Christian context. But Eddie was their brother, and his normal enthusiasm was at a high level about this man, David Hogan. The guys weren't about to disappoint him. They had been planning a trip to see Eddie anyway, so they jumped in the car and made the short trip to Yuba City. What they experienced would change them forever. Their entire paradigm and belief in what was possible was about to be radically shifted.

David Hogan is a veteran missionary to the indigenous people of Central Mexico. He has spent a lifetime ministering in some of the darkest, most dangerous places imaginable. He raised his family there, and he has a number of people who are with him day and night, including a couple of sons-in-law. David has combated real evil face to face for decades and has seen miracles that few get to witness. To date, he has seen hundreds raised from the dead. Most of these miracles are well documented in eyewitness accounts from visiting pastors and everyday people. I have personally met him and heard him speak more than once. He is the real deal if there ever was one.

With an infectious authenticity, David is no showman and does not care if you like him, his style, or his appearance. He comes to report and testify to the goodness of God and is unlike the typical TV evangelist. He has no flash and puts on no show. He is a "nothing but the facts, ma'am," type of guy. This man full of the Holy Spirit and walks in tremendous power that oozes from every pore. He is a Jesus man through and through and does nothing he does not hear the Father tell Him to do.

David spoke in his typical, fiery, good-old-boy tone about the things he had witnessed and done partnering with the Holy Spirit in his work with the people God has given him to reach and shepherd. He told stories about demons, witchcraft, warlocks, and downright hostile people trying to kill him and his crew. He talked about the miracles and all the victories he has had through God's Holy Spirit. He spoke about surviving shots from arrows and bullets and about whole villages coming to Christ after witnessing miraculous healings and resurrections from the dead!

His words penetrated Joaquin and Jahi like hot swords. They felt as if David was speaking directly to them despite there being a thousand or more souls in the hall. When he talked about giving up a sinful lifestyle and submitting to the call of Christ, Jahi felt as if David was looking into his soul.

Then David said, "Don't feel that the Holy Spirit can't reveal to me what's in your hearts!"

The boys were becoming completely convicted. They felt the rightness of all he said and knew they needed to make changes in their lives.

When Joaquin tells this story he explains, "For me, at that moment, it was not as much a sin conviction, although that is definitely part of it. It was more the conviction that God was real and Christ was real and Christianity was not just a religion but a relationship with the living Christ."

The guys were sitting halfway back in the middle of the sanctuary. Immediately, they both stood and hastily began making their way down the center aisle toward the stage. It was a surreal moment for them, as both were experiencing high emotions. As he approached the stage, Joaquin remembers clearly, "It was almost like I was detached from my body, watching myself respond."

At this point, Hogan paused for a moment, apparently preparing to make an altar call (calling people forward to make a commitment to Jesus Christ). Eddie's account was that before Hogan could get the words out of his mouth, both Joaquin and Jahi had hurried from their seats and had gotten all the way up front to the stage! Eddie says David growled in his Alabama drawl, "What do you two want?"

All the boys could say was, "Jesus!"

Joaquin remembers thinking, "Whatever it is you have, I want it!"

In David Hogan, they saw someone who had a real, palpable relationship with the living God and had power flowing through his life, and they wanted it! Joaquin and Jahi had never known Christianity could be this real. This was something two bold, adventurous, tough-minded young men like these two could sink their teeth into.

David prayed and led them both to Jesus. Then, he went on to give an altar call with dozens more coming forward for salvation.

To say our sons were changed is an understatement. That experience at Glad Tidings Church was a landmark event for them and, as it turns out, for us, their parents, as well. Many years later, I was able to thank David personally after he spoke at Bethel Church in Redding, California. But David Hogan was just one of many who have had an important part to play in our spiritual growth. Many have contributed by praying for us, teaching us, mentoring us, and just plain loving on us and sharing their lives with us. They all have had a hand in getting the Evans family to where we are in our journey today.

JOAQUIN

The encounter with David Hogan was just the beginning for the boys. A little over a year later, Joaquin experienced another supernatural encounter at a Christian youth camp. Eddie was scheduled to help with the camp sponsored by his church. At the last minute, he invited Joaquin to come with him and serve as a counselor. There, God encountered Joaquin in a manner that once again confirmed to my son of the immense truth that God is real.

At each night and morning service, Joaquin sat in the back repeating the same prayer, "God, if You are real, do something!"

During the third service on the second night, praying the same prayer with a genuine hunger to know the reality of God, he heard an inner audible voice that said, "You need to be humble."

Joaquin then prayed what he now knows is a very dangerous prayer: "Humble me."

Then, he heard God say, "You need to get low."

Joaquin lowered his chin to his chest.

"Lower."

He bent over.

"You need to get lower."

He sat down.

"Lower."

He put his head between his knees.

In a stern but loving voice, God said, "You're still not low enough."

At this point, Joaquin realized God wanted him to fully surrender, to lie prostrate before Him. He thought to himself, "God I don't want to get down on the floor in front of all these teenagers!"

Joaquin hadn't been paying much attention to what was going on around him up until then. Suddenly, he heard the speaker say that at exactly one year prior to this meeting, to the day, God spoke to him in his bedroom and said, "This generation is going to be the captains of the Army of the Final Harvest."

At that word, Joaquin experienced the heavens break open! Liquid love began descending from heaven like molasses, tangible liquid love flowing down through his body. Then God said, once again in a stern but loving voice, "You're still not low enough."

At this point, the pastor stopped his message and said he felt God was telling him that there were some people who needed to come forward and humble themselves on the floor before God. No one moved. Joaquin realized the pastor was speaking to him. But after pausing a second and seeing no one move, the pastor went on speaking.

Joaquin wondered by not coming forward if he had missed his opportunity. He said to God, "If that was You, have him say it again."

He repeated this prayer three times. On the third repetition, the speaker stopped abruptly and said more sternly, "No! God is saying that people need to come and humble themselves on the floor before Him right now!"

Joaquin knew that meant him. He jumped up and ran to the front with a bunch of young people. As soon as Joaquin knelt to his knees and lay face-first on the ground, he knew that was what God had been waiting for. What had started as love slowly leaking over him broke into a waterfall of God's love falling over him and through him.

As this magnificent love encounter continued, the pastor stopped praying for the others, walked over behind Joaquin where he lay prostrate on the floor, and began to prophesy over him. He was so caught up in what he was experiencing at the moment that he doesn't remember what the pastor said, but he does remember the supernatural event he experienced next.

While lying in a fetal position on the ground, crying and being undone by the Lord, Joaquin was taken into a vision. In this vision, he was standing in a body of water. Looking out before him, it was so vast it appeared to have no end. As he glanced to his right and saw Jesus standing behind him on the bank. Jesus motioned to the water and said, "This is My presence. Right now you are standing only ankle-deep, but you can have as much as you want."

As Jesus made this proclamation, a wave of life-giving energy came out of Him and penetrated through Joaquin's body. In retrospect, Joaquin now feels this was a personal commission to pursue the presence of Jesus!

Jesus went on to say, "This is My presence, and there is enough here for anyone who has ever wanted Me to have as much as they'd like."

As He spoke these words, another wave of life-giving energy emanated from Him and went through my son. Joaquin felt this was another commission, this time to invite people into this place of experiencing the depths of His love and His presence.

Joaquin then found himself back on the floor, in the same fetal position, crying. He also heard God give him clear instructions to "GO find that kid from the day before!"

One of the kids at the camp was a young gangbanger who had been sent there in hopes that he'd start making better choices. He clearly did not want to be there and had been making his desire to leave very evident. He had given another young camper a hard time, cursing and threatening, putting his street toughness on full display. Joaquin, who wasn't on the camp's staff, but was there solely as a guest, instinctively stepped in and intervened for the young camper, who was clearly facing a situation he was ill-equipped to handle. Joaquin had had a serious face-to-face conversation with the gangbanger, which seemed to calm him down some, but he still wasn't having any of this Christian stuff.

The last thing Joaquin wanted to do just now was to leave the most peaceful, bliss-filled moment of his life to go talk to that troubled kid. He told God he wanted to stay in that euphoric bliss of His presence. However, if you know your Bible, you know people seldom win arguments with God. So, Joaquin got up, spotted the kid on the back row of the room, approached him, and without thinking too much about it, put his hand on the young man's shoulder. As he did so, he began to feel everything the young man was feeling and started to prophesy over him. He told him about his life, his past, and, more importantly, his future and what he was called to do with his life.

As this young man started to become completely undone, the grace Joaquin had been granted while experiencing God's presence began to lift, and it struck him that he didn't know what he was doing! Joaquin left the young man with some of the camp counselors, who continued to minister to him, while he went away for several hours to enter back into life-changing interaction with the Lord.

God had just given Joaquin his first real assignment, one of many to come!

JAHI

Meanwhile, Jahi had moved back home to Camarillo with us. Despite having had that power experience at the David Hogan meeting, he had begun to slip back into his old lifestyle. He was partying a lot, hanging out with his friends, and doing unhealthy things that twenty-year-olds sometimes do with their friends in their spare time. He was having fun, going to a local college, and exploring life, but there was something missing, a void inside that none of those activities were capable of filling. He remembered that power encounter and wanted more. He wanted to know if God was real! He was tired of running hard and fast but getting nowhere. Our son wanted more in his life, so he began to read his Bible and pray.

If you've tried to read the Bible as a new believer, you know it can be a daunting task. It was no different for us and many others I know. It certainly was no different for my son. However, everything changed when he prayed a prayer of surrender to God and verbally committed all he had to the Lord. Isolated in his upstairs bedroom, Jahi had a visitation from God's Holy Spirit. The Spirit began to explain the Scriptures to him. He walked him through very difficult passages that Jahi was struggling with, and spent several nights with Jahi explaining the Bible and many other mysteries of the kingdom of God to him.

Many people report an almost supernatural ability to understand Scripture once they've said the Sinner's Prayer (a prayer of recognition that Jesus is the promised Messiah, the Son of God, and was crucified for the forgiveness of sin for all who claim Him as Lord and King). The baptism of the Holy Spirit (an actual experience of the Holy Spirit bathing you in His presence) is unique for each individual, but it is something all Christians need to seek for empowerment to walk in spiritual authority. Jahi was in the presence of God's Holy Spirit in a way that is difficult to explain but is unique and unlike anything else you will ever experience! One who has had such an encounter knows exactly what we mean!

During this time with the Holy Ghost—I believe it may have been the morning after the first visitation—Jahi entered the kitchen where Paula and I were having breakfast. I was sitting with my back to the kitchen entrance when he entered. Immediately, I felt a very strong presence behind me—that's the only way I can describe it. I looked up at my wife and saw a look of awe and puzzlement on her face. She looked as if someone she knew had just walked into the room, but the person had just had major plastic surgery or something. She looked like she knew the person yet didn't know them.

I turned around to see why she was looking so perplexed and immediately saw why. It was our son, and yet it wasn't! He was wearing a facial expression I'd never seen before. Jahi, to this point, could be very moody, sometimes a bit sullen. Again, we were all black belts and competed fairly regularly (except for Paula who, though a black belt, had competed only once in a martial arts competition). Jahi often carried himself like he was about to step into the ring for an all-out brawl any minute.

It wasn't just a change in Jahi's facial expression. There was a glow about him that almost took my breath away. Our son was being transformed, "born again." We both said "good morning" to him, and he just smiled, grabbed his cereal, and proceeded back to his upstairs room.

My wife and I looked at each other and simultaneously asked, "Who was that?"

Weeks passed before Jahi revealed to us the details of this encounter. A supernatural occurrence like this one can be deeply personal to the person experiencing it and also very hard to explain. To say this experience changed the course of his life would be a huge understatement. At the time, our son was being watched very closely by USA officials for a spot on the USA Taekwondo Olympic Team. Instead, he went on to become a missionary and to marry a beautiful Messianic Jewish (believes in Jesus) girl named Kes. Believing parents raised Kes and her brothers and sisters to walk in the ways of our Lord Jesus Christ and to be amazing worship leaders. Jahi and Kes regularly teach on the importance of Israel and the Jewish people in God's plan for total redemption and the return of Jesus Christ.

CHAPTER 17

UNCONDITIONAL SURRENDER

After watching our two sons completely transform into people we barely recognized, Paula and I began to think there might be something to this Christianity thing. Both had been tough, determined young men, tough on the football field and in the martial arts ring. They never lost their toughness, but now they possessed a strong tenderness that was hard to explain. If anything, they became even stronger and more focused, as if they knew a secret no one else knew.

Soon after Jahi's experience, Joaquin visited us in Camarillo. He called ahead, saying he had something very important to share with us. His purpose, as it turned out, was to share the gospel of Jesus Christ with his parents. He wanted us to know for sure that God is real and heaven is a real place.

He was clearly transformed, and his delivery was so genuine and powerful that we had to take notice. Later, he told me he was very nervous when he arrived at our house. He knew we had been very skeptical about Christianity and, until the recent past, had been into New Age philosophy. What we saw was not a nervous person, far from it. He looked like a young man under the influence of some powerful drug! He was extremely mellow and calm. In my mind he looked like what I thought a true far-eastern yogi would look like. This was not the tough-minded, strong young man we had raised. Don't get me wrong—he didn't come off as weak at all, just super mellow.

Paula and I listened intently, but just as we had experienced with Jahi, we were struck more by what we saw than what we heard. We both knew we had to start re-thinking our priorities and re-examining the direction of our lives. While we thought we were doing okay, we were obviously missing something big!

I began to read the old King James Bible we had at the house and started to "talk" to Jesus, mostly in the shower. I wouldn't call it prayer just yet. I don't know why, just pride or stubbornness or something, but those were the beginning steps for me. For the next few weeks, we had people over to the house we knew were also seeking answers and were curious. These were odd meetings, with a mixture of New Age stuff we all had learned and new discoveries we were making about Christianity. These discussions were lively and very interesting for a few weeks, but soon lost their promise of yielding anything of real value.

Next, we began to visit various churches: Baptist, Pentecostal, Church of Christ, new start-ups, and other denominations. Nothing seemed to give us what we were looking for—a power encounter like our sons had experienced. Nothing earth-shattering happened in any of these meetings.

But, things were starting to happen. Believers will tell you God seems to orchestrate the early believer's growth in spectacular ways. In the beginning, fantastic, supernatural things seem to happen to let new believers know God is real and present. It's like God wants to show off for you—He wants to "seal the deal" so to speak. Crazy, almost impossible stuff starts to happen, and outlandish prayers are answered.

I was riding down the freeway one day when I told my wife I had just told God, if He was real, to give me the teal-colored, 4-wheel-drive Ford Explorer I just saw on a billboard. I also asked Him to bring me a new job making $60,000 a year with flexible hours that would allow me to teach full-time at my dojang, keep my part-time faculty position at Ventura College, and continue to travel the country with my competition teams. Pretty crazy stuff, but God went right to work.

I made these "prayers" on a Sunday. The next day, I had a very strong prompting to call a friend in Orange County who owned several home health agencies. Home health was a business I knew very well since I had been part owner and CEO of one for several years before selling it in 1996. My friend's name was Marilynn, and to my surprise she said, "I was just about to call you. I have an agency in the Valley near Northridge that is hemorrhaging money. If I can't get it turned around soon, I'm going to have to sell it or close it. Can you help me?"

By Wednesday, I was in Anaheim meeting with Marilynn, who offered me a position overseeing the agency at $50,000 per year. I felt I could get the $60k per year I had asked the Lord for if I pressed in, but because I knew she was in dire straits, I didn't want to take advantage. Besides, she'd already agreed to all my other conditions: I could work as much or as little as I wanted, I was to receive full benefits, and I had full control to hire and fire as I saw fit. I countered with $55,000, and she accepted.

God had come through, big time! But what about the Explorer?

I started working for Marilynn's company in April of 2001. We began to turn things around, and the company's bottom line started looking better. In early August, I received a phone call from Marilynn's husband—I'll call him E—asking my opinion on a large purchase he was planning to make. In order to get to some of our remote patients (usually the wealthier ones), our nurses had to travel some pretty nasty back roads. Many didn't have vehicles sturdy enough to get the job done, so he proposed getting Ford Focuses for the nursing staff.

Immediately, I felt God smile. Just like when I heard His voice in jail, I knew what was coming. That Ford Explorer was about to be mine. I advised E to get something bigger and sturdier, not out of manipulation, but because it just made sense based upon the circumstances and the roads I knew our nurses had to manage. E decided to go back to the Ford dealer to see what sort of deal he could work. A few days later I got another call. E had worked out a pretty good deal with the dealership for 4-wheel-drive Explorers!

While the deal was good, it was also costly. I felt another check from the Lord and told E we didn't need 4-wheel-drives. The Explorer's ground clearance was sufficient for our needs; we didn't need the extra equipment. He agreed and went back to make the deal.

To this point, there was no mention of me getting one of these vehicles, but I knew it was coming. A few weeks earlier, I had found a major error the company's young, inexperienced accountant had made in the firm's financials. Marilyn was desperate to secure a loan to save the company, but the bank had repeatedly denied her. Presented with a fresh set of corrected financials, the bank approved her loan, securing the much-needed influx of cash. In addition, our branch was turning around and was now making a profit.

Two days later, I received another call from E telling me he had made a deal to lease several Ford Explorers, and one had been assigned to me. I was excited to get the new SUV, but what excited me more was that God had demonstrated His love for me in such an obvious and dramatic fashion. He even arranged for me to play a part in the decision-making process leading to the procurement of the vehicles. I hadn't even known E four months earlier when I prayed that prayer.

I got a call from the main office the next day. The office manager informed me I could come down and pick up the Explorer any time, but she suggested I come right away to get the pick of the color I wanted. I laughed to myself, knowing what color my SUV would be.

I waited two days before going down. When I arrived, there was only one vehicle left sitting across the street from the office in the Safeway parking lot. The office manager jokingly said the staff was beginning to wonder if I wanted it. She offered to have someone show me to the car, but I politely refused help, stating I was confident I could find it on my own. She gave me a quizzical look and reluctantly said, "Okay."

I took the keys and walked across the street to the Safeway lot. Beside the one Explorer our company owned, there were two other Explorers parked in that lot. I had the keys to the car, but this was before the advent of the electronic automobile key fob, so there were no buttons to push to identify which one of them was mine. I didn't need it. Sitting in a space facing in the direction of our office was the exact same 2001 Ford Explorer I had seen on that billboard back in April. It was the exact same color with the same wheels and hubs. It was perfect, and I knew it was my gift from Him. I walked up to that SUV, confidently stuck the key in the lock, and without a hitch, the door smoothly opened. I smiled, took a deep breath, and stepped up into my promise!

HOLY SPIRIT CAME

Two weeks later, I received an invitation from Eddie to attend a men's winter retreat sponsored by his church, Glad Tidings, in Yuba City. David Hogan was supposed to be the guest speaker—yes, the same David Hogan who changed the course of our two sons' lives. Of course, I said yes without a second's hesitation. I had to meet and hear the man who had impacted my family in such a dramatic way. No way was I going to miss this opportunity,

The men's retreat was to take place at a campsite in the Sierra Mountains featuring several cabins that housed up to a dozen men and two huge Quonset huts that served as a dining hall and a meeting room. Somewhere around seventy-five to a hundred men had signed up to attend.

Jahi and I planned to drive up on September 12, 2001. The day before we left, the entire world came to a horrific standstill as we watched two jetliners crash into the World Trade Centers in New York City and a third near the Pentagon in Washington, DC. No one knew what was going to happen next. Would there be more attacks? Would the country retaliate? Was someone going to drop "the bomb"? We all collectively held our breath.

My wife's niece and a friend had dropped in for a visit on their way home to Oregon and had planned to leave on 9/11. We held them back a day just to make sure they would be safe to travel. Receiving word from Glad Tidings the camp was still a go, we made preparations to leave the following day. All flights had been grounded, so Jahi and I drove the girls to a nearby town where they could catch a non-stop bus to Portland and wouldn't have to transfer, thus cutting down the odds of dealing with anything unsavory due to current events. After seeing them on their bus, we headed to Northern California and our new adventure. My anticipation was sky-high.

We arrived at the camp in the early evening in time for the dinner bell and met Eddie and Joaquin. Everyone was excited and our expectation for what God was going to do over the next few days was elevating by the hour. Then word came flights had been grounded out of Mexico. Unless David Hogan had already flown in, we knew that meant he would not make it. We heard he was still trying to make his way to us, determined to get to our camp if it was humanly possible. However, by Thursday afternoon, we got word it was not going to happen. Despite David's best efforts, all transport had been brought to a standstill. The nation was on high alert, and the government was taking no chances. At least we found out the girls had made it home safely to Portland, some consoling news.

All was not lost. David Kiteley, a pastor from Shiloh Church, a well-known charismatic church in Oakland, California, agreed to come to the camp. David proved to be a dynamic and inspiring speaker. He delivered the Word of God with power, knowledge, intellect, and humor, and I thoroughly enjoyed him.

After David spoke, I left the meeting room feeling like the camp was going to be just what I needed. Even though I was not going to meet the amazing David Hogan, I still had a few days to escape from a very busy schedule and the crazy demands required to run Premier Martial Arts, the home health agency branch, and my teaching assignments at Ventura College. Between Premier and the college, I had over three hundred students, who came with a ton of interpersonal junk that would take me another book to cover. Yet there was something still missing. I felt a very unfamiliar stirring in my spirit. There was something I needed to be doing or pursuing, but I had no idea what that might be.

Late that evening, I walked into the sanctuary to a strange scene. I saw men down on their knees crying out to God. Some were shedding actual tears, some calling out in desperation, and others silently facing the wall, lips moving in obvious prayer and petition. A few of these men were the same guys who had been talking smack and throwing elbows during a few games of basketball we had played that afternoon. These weren't soft men. Some were rough-handed plumbers, carpenters, and construction workers. Some I knew to be black belts from a local school in Yuba City whose master instructor was a friend of mine. I respected these guys, and all in all, it was a pretty tough bunch. But here they all were, in total submission to the Lord, laying their thoughts, problems, desires, and innermost secrets out before Him.

Then it struck me. That's what was missing, the thing I needed to do! I realized my pride was hindering me from receiving heaven's best. My pride required me to hold something back and not submit to any man or any thing, including God. True, I had started to read my Bible again, and my wife and I had tried a few churches around town. I had even started praying again, and God had revealed Himself to me in magnificent ways. I had seen Him completely transform my sons and witnessed miraculous answers to outrageous prayers, yet I still hadn't let Him into my heart, not completely.

John the Baptist said he must decrease so the Messiah could increase (John 3:30). I think many would-be believers, myself included, initially have this idea that fully surrendering our lives to Christ will cause us to decrease and diminish in some way. In fact, the opposite is true. John the Baptist prepared the way for Jesus' ministry, so it was appropriate for him to step back when Jesus took center stage. But Jesus, who is the Head of His church and body, does not require us to diminish to bring Him glory. Rather, He wants us to increase in Him so that we can put His glory on full display! However, for us to grow and become His authorized ambassadors here on earth and for Him to use us for maximum impact in this fallen and dying world, He first needs our total commitment.

Right then and there in the sanctuary surrounded by men crying out to God, I realized I was not giving my all to Him. Not even close. I was making the same mistake so many nominal, lukewarm believers make. I wanted God on my terms, not His, and folks, it just doesn't work that way. As committed believers we must surrender to God's will, not our own! "His will must be done on Earth, as it is heaven" (Matthew 6:10 One New Man). God needs people who are surrendered to Him, so His will may be done on this earth. He gave us free will. Free means liberty, and He gave us liberty and a magnificent brain so we might discern truth from lie and make the ultimate decision to follow Him or not. Think about it. A parent wants their child to learn the basic principles about life from them. It's their job—not the TV's, the street's, or even the school system's. It is the parent's job to teach their children how to live and thrive in this world. God is no different. Matthew 7 teaches that God is the best parent there is. No human parent can compare. But we must choose to trust and follow Him as our Father and teacher.

The moment I realized this, I knew what I must do. I had to surrender to Him. I had tried doing life on my terms without Him and had been moderately successful, but there was still an unfilled void inside, a tangible emptiness in my spirit. I looked at those strong men, and I knew I had to abandon pride—at least the kind of pride keeping me from true intimacy with Him. This kind of pride makes a man tell himself he needs no one else and keeps him separated from his Creator.

Those men didn't care what I thought, only what God thought. Without realizing it, I had not fully given myself to God due to fear—the fear of getting hurt if I gave up control to someone else. Submitting my will to someone else would make me vulnerable, leaving me without my false armor of protection, the illusion I was in control of anything. I had worked hard to build that illusion and had run far away from that little kid who felt alone and unprotected on the streets of DC. I hadn't recognized there is actually more protection for an individual surrounded by people who love him or her than an individual attempting to stand alone. What greater love is there than the love of God?

Suddenly, I didn't care what anyone else thought. I had to do this, whatever it was. Right on that spot, in the Sierra mountains, at a Christian men's camp, on September 13, 2001, I again confessed my sins to the Lord, asked forgiveness, and told Him He could have all of me and everything I owned. I surrendered my will, ambitions, present, and future to Jesus. I sincerely said, "Take it all but just give me more of You!"

What happened next was both strange and unexpected. A feeling began to creep into my consciousness. At first, I felt a tremendous weight lift off me, like I had suddenly lost fifty pounds. Then, I began to experience a slight sense of euphoria. The combination of the two was overwhelming. My legs went limp, and I dropped to my knees. I don't remember falling further, but the next thing I knew I was on my face crying like a three-year-old. The tears were tears of release, as if fifty years of pain and anger were draining out of me, or more accurately, like they were being drawn out of me. I do not know how long I was on that floor, maybe twenty minutes or even two hours. I don't know, but I do know I felt like a completely empty vessel. I felt lighter than air. It's a good thing no one suggested I could fly right then because I might have gone to the nearest ledge and tried it.

I woke up the next morning feeling better than I had in years. We went to breakfast in the dining hall, and as I sat with my family eating, I noticed a man sitting several tables away staring at me. He wasn't just looking in my direction occasionally; his gaze never wavered, though his eyes projected no threat. It was as if he was observing and contemplating something unusual, familiar but rare.

At the next meal, the same thing happened. This fellow just kept staring, and this time he was positioned so he could have a better view. I know this sounds creepy and almost perverse, but I didn't get the feeling my observer was motivated by anything dark. He just seemed to be curious, like he was studying me. People were trying to talk to him, but he was pretty much ignoring everyone around him. He just kept his gaze locked upon me.

After lunch, I got up to leave the hall, and I couldn't help but notice this man follow me out. He was a few steps behind me when someone came up to him and started to speak to him. "Go away!" he said. "Can't you see I'm busy?"

The sharpness of his tone made me turn and look at him, and what I saw was the most disturbing part of this very strange day. My observant friend was behind me, literally bending at the waist trying to see my face with an odd intensity of expression that was downright unsettling. The man who had come up to ask him a question was walking away with a very wounded look on his face. The thought occurred to me this guy may be disturbed, but why would they allow him to participate in this men's camp? He was obviously someone important. You could tell by the gaggle of people he always had around him; however, at this moment I didn't care. I picked up my pace and beelined it to my quarters and my bunk to read.

But I couldn't read. The feeling of euphoria continued to grow with each passing hour and couldn't be ignored. I was higher than any drug I'd ever taken. Something strange and wonderful was happening to me. I couldn't explain it and had no grid for it. It would be a long time before Joaquin and Jahi shared their Holy

Spirit encounters with me, so I didn't have their experiences as a reference. It was all new and unknown territory for me. I soon forgot about my admiring friend as I went deeper into this place of total peace. I had never felt so good in my life.

After dinner, I pointed out to Eddie the man that had shown so much interest in me and asked who he was. Eddie told me his name and said he was a famous prophet connected to the church sponsoring our retreat. Eddie said not to worry about his behavior, because he was eccentric like that. Eddie also said if this prophet was showing that much interest in me, he must have been seeing something in the spirit regarding me. Remember, I was raised in a Southern Baptist church for the most part, although a significant number of my extended family were Methodist, with a smattering of Catholics. I had no grid for prophets or "seeing in the spirit." This was all too strange for me, but I was so "high" I didn't care.

The prophet's name was Paul. Eddie had traveled abroad with Paul on an extended ministry trip and knew him well. Eddie told me quite a bit about him. Evidently, his prophetic gift was very strong. I later concluded that, in the spirit, he could see Holy Spirit working in me! His eccentricity was on full display as he awkwardly followed me after our meal, staring at me without saying a word.

I was high and getting higher. High as in intoxicated. As you know by now, I knew what it was to feel high. I began smoking marijuana and hashish in high school with my friends. When I got to California at twenty-one years old, I started getting and staying high on weed, cocaine, acid, and occasionally heroin. I only snorted heroin, but I'd do just about anything I could smoke, snort, or swallow. By the age of thirty, I was strung out smoking crack cocaine, until I finally hit bottom. This thing I was experiencing on that mountaintop was so far beyond anything I had ever experienced before in my life. There literally was no comparison. It was not just a good high—it was an intense, joyful experience, like being in a barrel of liquid love.

I realize now the key element in my family's testimony is "surrender." Joaquin's breakthrough, Jahi's breakthrough, and mine all came after we wholeheartedly, with no reservations, surrendered ourselves to the lordship of Jesus Christ. (Paula's experience came a little while later.) Scripture tells us those who surrender to the sovereignty of Christ are "sealed by the Holy Spirit." I believe this is exactly what happened to us. Jesus told Nicodemus in John 3 that one must be "born again" to enter into the kingdom of heaven. I believe we were all born again!

I stayed in that state of euphoria for twenty-eight days! I was a wreck. I hardly slept and came close to killing myself a couple of times on my hour commute to the San Fernando Valley for work. I was in such a state of bliss I'd miss turns or just drift off the freeway onto the shoulder. The sound of gravel hitting the side of my brand-new Explorer would jar me back to semi-alertness, a couple of times just in time to avoid hitting overpass abutments. At the office, I remember trying to settle disputes between co-workers by telling them to just love each other. As you can imagine, that didn't go over very well.

I had a difficult time staying focused enough to teach my martial arts classes. It just didn't make sense to me teaching people how to hurt each other. I couldn't reconcile it, plus I just felt too good. I'd be teaching a pretty aggressive advanced adult class and would suddenly stop, pausing to reflect on how beautiful my students looked. My students were pretty good about it all. They'd continue on with their drills, giving me a curious look or two every now and again. Jahi, who was my chief instructor at the time, totally got it and would intervene by taking class over when needed. He did the same at weekly staff meetings when I would suddenly zone out.

My poor wife was beside herself. First her two boys, now her husband. Paula didn't know what to make of any of it until the Holy Spirit accosted her a few months later, in January. For twenty-eight days, she had to put up with me not sleeping, not eating, and practically not communicating, at least coherently anyway. She would wake up in the middle of the night to find me in another room listening to contemporary Christian music, crying as I swayed back and forth. Or she'd find me in an upstairs bedroom on the floor talking to the Holy Spirit (who she could not see).

Paula is a black belt, a wife, and a mother, but she is also a very skilled and experienced medical professional. As a registered nurse who had served in just about every professional capacity in her career, from the emergency room to mental health nursing, she was stumped as to what to do with me. She was completely baffled by what was happening to me. It was very unnerving for her. Her three rocks appeared to be crumbling.

But we weren't crumbling. Just the opposite. We were experiencing the most amazing physical and spiritual state a human being can be in. We were completely wrapped up in God's perfect love and were being loved on so intensely by the King of the universe that everything else would, from time to time, just fade away.

CHAPTER 18

HE WANTED US ALL

In my naiveté, I was convinced every believer experienced what I was going through. After all, my boys had very similar encounters and experiences. Why was this thing such a well-kept secret? Why didn't all my Christian friends tell me it could be like this?

Most Christians I knew were really nice folks that we loved but, for the most part, just tolerated. They had tried their best to share their faith with us, but nothing they said ever found its mark. They would talk about the love of Christ and how life could be really great following Jesus, but it all just sounded like nice empty words. We were action-oriented people. I had spent years studying the supernatural, both on my own and at Sonoma State University, and had seen and witnessed many things, starting with encounters in an alleged haunted house while I was in college in Nebraska, then hearing that Voice in jail, and the out-of-body experience in Berkeley (and no, I wasn't on an acid trip). I believed in the spirit realm and had seen and witnessed too much not to believe, but a singular God capable of this much love and intimacy was completely surprising and unexpected.

If my Christian friends had told us about this, we would have signed up years earlier. My family and I weren't special. We didn't have any attributes that would cause the Creator of all things to turn His magnificence on us. So, everyone must experience this, whatever it was, when they made the plunge, right? But then, why did I see so many people with crucifixes around their necks fighting and bickering? If every believer was immersed in this glory, why was there so much animosity amongst denominations and people who claimed to believe? I just didn't get it. It made no sense to me. Could it be every believer didn't experience this? Could there be people who had really surrendered to His sovereignty but were denied this intense love? Or were most people who claimed to be followers of Christ just the way I had been a few short weeks ago just talking the talk but not walking the walk? Could most believers still be holding onto their way instead of His way? I had to know, so I began to watch and observe.

As the days passed into weeks, I found it more difficult to function normally. Driving was difficult, sleeping was difficult, managing my everyday affairs was difficult, and most of all, giving a good damn about anything the world had to offer was increasingly difficult. I soon began to realize if I stayed in this state, I could very well lose my jobs, because my bosses didn't care about my sudden love affair with a man named Jesus. I also slowly realized most people jammed into church every Sunday had no idea what a true encounter with God was like.

Now I did, and I was afraid I might not survive it. I so appreciated God giving me this taste of heaven. I was changed forever, born again. I didn't care what great arguments anyone presented to me or what logic the best philosophers and atheistic theorists threw my way. There would be no unconvincing me, no turning me around. I was a lifer. I had tasted and seen the goodness of the Lord. No argument would ever hold sway over me. Once you'd seen, held, and felt a basketball, no one could ever convince you that basketballs (at least one) don't exist. It was a simple as this: I had seen and believed and could not be told differently.

So, I said the words, "Lord, please lift this off of me! Though I love it, I don't think I can function in this world any longer like this."

Within moments, I began to feel the change. The heaviness didn't return, but the pure ecstasy I'd been experiencing started to lift. Some part of me knew I had to return fully to this world and begin to tend to my responsibilities more efficiently, but a large part of me regretted that decision, even to this day. It was the correct thing to do, but it hurt.

I believe it is partly what the author of Hebrews meant when he admonished believers to grow and develop in the faith. He said at some point one must get off of breast milk and graduate to solid food (Hebrews 5:12-14). One's faith and convictions must be grounded in the knowledge that God is very good and has a plan for us all (Jeremiah 29:11), not in luxuriating in a constant state of intoxication (though He does allow me back there every now and again. Like I said, He is good!).

Despite the shift, there was one thing I knew—I was not abandoned. I knew I could commune with the Holy Spirit whenever I wanted to. All I had to do was turn my attention back to Him, and He would come. As a matter of fact, I have felt His presence several times while writing this book. I can experience that same feeling (His presence) almost as intensely while in worship, reading the Word, or just spending time thinking of Him.

In case anyone is wondering, I was never, nor am I now, brainwashed. I've studied psychology extensively, completing both my bachelor's and master's degrees with an additional year of post-graduate clinical training. I'd know if I had been subjected to any mind manipulation at the men's camp or at any other time. I was not! My experience was genuine. While you may not agree with the cause of it all, don't doubt the experience for a moment.

A few months after my twenty-eight-day experience, in January 2002, Paula and I returned to Glad Tidings in Yuba City to meet with a famous deliverance pastor there named Jess Parker. Pastors specializing in this area have a gift to discern spirits and are trained to set a believer free of any unhealthy spiritual attachments. I made the appointment, and though I was skeptical about the whole concept, we fasted for three days as instructed, then made the eight-hour drive north. I wasn't sure why I needed it, but I was beginning to get a rudimentary understanding about the spirit world. People I trusted said it would be good for me, so off we went.

When we arrived, we found out Pastor Jess had been called away on an emergency and had assigned one of the deliverance pastors under him to meet with us. I was very nervous. I had been told a Christian could not be possessed by a demon, but I had also heard, under certain circumstances, demons could attach to and influence anyone. People will always have opinions, whether they know what they are talking about or not, and for some folks, opinions trump facts. I didn't know what to expect. Would I be embarrassed? I had done some pretty dark things in my life, things I was not proud of. Would all of my past evil deeds be exposed? Would this pastor judge me?

Paula wanted to come with me, and deep down I was relieved. I welcomed having her support. The pastor was a tall, very friendly young man, who appeared to be around thirty. He projected an air of ease and confidence, and I began to relax as we exchanged a few pleasantries and got to know each other.

We entered into prayer at his suggestion. While we were praying, the pastor asked the Holy Spirit to give him insight into me and words of knowledge and wisdom. This was the first time I had heard about these spiritual gifts (see 1 Corinthians 12). When we were done praying, he looked at me and began to "read my mail." This young man was telling me things about myself he couldn't possibly know. He talked about my childhood—the good, the bad, and the ugly. He even knew where I grew up and talked about my struggles and my triumphs. Most importantly, he told me I had no demonic presence about me, and heaven had a plan and purpose for my life. His words brought back to remembrance the Voice that spoke to me in jail: "We are not done with you yet!"

What seemed like a half an hour session actually lasted over two and a half hours. It was another life-changing experience in a growing list of life-changing events I had been experiencing. I was awed and curious at the same time. Did God really speak that clearly to people? Was this young pastor someone especially ordained by God? What was the trick? What did he have to do to get this gift—fast forty days, live like a hermit on a snow-covered mountaintop in a cave for a year? At this point in my young Christian life, I had more questions than answers. One thing was clear, though—pursuing the deeper things of God was far from boring.

As we headed back to Eddie Tait's family home where we were staying, I noticed something a little different with my wife. When I asked her what was going on with her, she answered that what she had just witnessed opened something up in her. This is what she remembers in her own words:

Jim had scheduled a "deliverance" with a pastor at Glad Tidings. He had followed the instructions and fasted for the prior three days. I was not sure what was expected of me or if I would even be able to be involved. I knew very little about the process. Once we got to

Yuba City, we were told I would be able to be in the session but just as an observer. Still not knowing what part I would play, I decided to partner with Jim and fast until his scheduled session.

Jim's session started in the morning and lasted for about two and a half hours, at least that's my memory of the day. It started with a man introducing himself and letting Jim know the point of deliverance was to go for the "root" of issues, things that may have been introduced unknowingly or knowingly in the past and may have caused lasting negative effects.

The session remains somewhat of a blur to me, but I do remember his digging into Jim's past. He went after incidents that had made Jim feel "less than." He dug into times he received mixed messages from the adult role models in his life that led to confusion. Going to church and hearing one thing and then being told after a fight with another kid "not to come back in until he had hit that kid." As the session continued, I saw a release and relief come over Jim.

My main memory of the event is I felt a tangible presence during Jim's deliverance and saw a real transformation in my husband. He was lighter and freer than I had ever seen him. It seemed that so many issues from childhood had come to the surface and had been removed by the "root." I remember the next day feeling lighter myself and being aware that there had been a real transformation in me. I didn't know exactly what had happened, but I knew we were both different. In retrospect I now know that I/we had encountered Holy Spirit.

It was days later before I realized my not-so-genteel language had cleaned up. Yes, I had developed the vocabulary of a sailor and had tried on multiple occasions over the years to clean it up without much success. During work one day, I realized I didn't swear anymore (Ephesians 4:29); in fact, it felt uncomfortable when I heard other people use profanity (a common occurrence where I worked). These events fueled an in-depth search for God's presence. We were desperate for more!

Paula had experienced the divine hand of God on a few occasions in her life prior to our deliverance that day, but just like so many of us, her previous encounters had not been enough to convince her to seek God.

One of those occurrences took place on a winding, mountainous portion of the famous Highway 1 in Northern California. It was 1984. I had been working at my new job in a psychiatric hospital in Bakersfield and Paula was finishing her nursing degree in Eureka. We decided she and the boys would catch a ride with a friend who was driving to Southern California for an appointment and join me for a weekend getaway at Disneyland. They would meet me in LA, and after our weekend treat, I would drive them all home.

On the way down, as they came around a blind curve in the road, they saw a young man in a one-ton pickup truck spread across both lanes of that narrow section of road. He had tried to do a U-turn in the road when his truck stalled. By the time the women realized what was happening, it was too late— there was no way to avoid the truck. On their right was a sheer mountain wall, and on their left was a drop-off down the side of the mountain to a rugged ravine below. The highway patrol estimated that their car was doing about fifty-five miles per hour when it slammed into the side of that young man's pickup.

Just before the impact of car against truck, Paula distinctly heard a voice telling her, "It's going to be alright!" It came out of nowhere and was completely reassuring. She instantly trusted that voice.

I got a call from the local authorities and rushed up to Ukiah, CA to find all four of them in the local hospital, banged up but okay.

Joaquin had been knocked unconscious and suffered damage to his right eye, Paula had severe pain across her chest where the seat belt restrained her, and Jahi was shaken but nothing seriously wrong. Paula's friend had a fracture to her chest area.

After checking on the family in the hospital and being assured they were okay, I went to look at the car. I was stunned when I walked up to the wreck they directed me to. I don't get stunned very easily. I thought there had to be a mistake. No one could have survived the mangled piece of metal I was looking at. The front of the car was crunched like an accordion. The roof was caved in so that there was no more than two and a half feet of headroom left in the front of the cabin. Paula said she remembered immediately jumping out of the car and snatching open the back door to check the kids. What I saw would have made that impossible. The passenger side door stood open about two inches. It was so damaged that I could not open it any further. Hard as I tried, I could not budge it another inch. Yet my wife managed to squeeze through that tiny opening to do whatever was needed to save our children.

The Voice was correct! It eventually was "going to be alright!"

Many years later on that day in January, witnessing my deliverance and experiencing the presence of God so intensely, Paula became convinced. She was now on-fire and desperate for more of God.

Now He had us all—Mama, Papa, and sons! It was as if the Holy Spirit gave us a small taste of what it is like to be in the presence of the purest of loves. He gave us all a small sample of what heaven must feel like.

We spent the next few years pursuing God any way we could. Paula, Jahi, and I found a solid Bible-teaching church, and we began to grow. We caught every lecture and conference we had the time and finances to attend. We surrounded ourselves with other Christians and picked the brains of any mature believers we could find.

CHAPTER 19

PRESSING IN

Our family spent the next few years satiating our enormous appetites for understanding more about God. We were pressing in on every front. Joaquin enrolled in Bethel Church's School of Supernatural Ministry (BSSM) in Redding, California, after discovering a growing gift for healing. Jahi was called to the mission field and went off to Cyprus to Gateways Beyond International's discipleship school (GTS). I had met the founder of the ministry, David Rudolph, on a ministry trip to the Ukraine. Jahi, coincidentally, had been to the Ukraine the year prior to my trip and had been very impressed with the leaders of a Messianic ministry there. David was speaking at a Messianic conference the year I was invited, and we were placed together as roommates. I learned about his ministry and the tremendous training program they ran on his home base in Cyprus. The focus of the Gateways' training school was to prepare missionaries of all ages and backgrounds to minister to the Jewish people the good news of Jesus Christ. Jahi loved the idea and enrolled.

Meanwhile, I enrolled in seminary in Los Angeles, while Paula and I became very active in Avenue Community Church in Ventura.

Before long, we were appointed as elders and were separately heading up several ministries. Paula's gift for intercession, as well as her gifts in administration and hospitality, grew by leaps and bounds. Her intercessory gift sprang to the forefront during our first trip to Israel. Soon after landing, she began demonstrating signs of distress and couldn't explain what was bothering her other than she felt pain in her spirit! None of us knew what that meant until we connected with Emma Rudolph, David Rudolph's wife. She and David were in Israel at the time. Emma has a strong intercessory gift and immediately recognized the same gift in Paula. Emma explained that Paula was feeling the spiritual pain of oppression so deeply implanted in this land. The pain of the Jewish people who have been oppressed by foreign conquerors for centuries, the pain of persecuted Christians, and the very pain suffered by our crucified Messiah run deep in the land. As Emma explained to Paula and the rest of our party the origins of her distress, it began to ease, and she slowly returned almost to her normal self, but there was a part of her that remained aware of that spiritual pain the entire trip. Emma then proceeded to take Paula's hands, and through prayer, imparted her impressive gift of intercession to Paula. What a gift!

It became clear to us that spiritual gifts were a real thing, that God, in His sovereignty and infinite wisdom, grants gifts and anointings to whomever He pleases, and that even we could have access to them. The Bible tells us there are gifts from the Father (1 Corinthians 12), the Son (Ephesians 4), and fruit from the Holy Spirit (Galatians 5). Joaquin was steadily growing in the gift of healing, Paula in intercession and others, and Jahi in the desire to see the good news spread to the nations through teaching and evangelism—all clearly heavenly gifts.

One day the Lord spoke the word revival to me. I knew the standard definition of revival. The root word is revive—to return to life, consciousness, vigor, strength, or a flourishing condition. However, I knew the Lord meant more than that, though I didn't know what.

By now, Joaquin was enrolled in the Bethel School of Supernatural Ministry, and we had been having very interesting conversations on many different theological, historical, and spiritual subjects. We talked about the textbooks we had in common in our different programs and also shared about the things we were learning in class such as historical Israel, the generals of the faith, the New Testament, the Old Testament, exegetics, and more. My program taught on the old movements of the Spirit from a historical perspective, but his BSSM program was teaching students how to live like revivalists today.

I needed to hear and learn how to live like a revivalist, because next God said to me, "I want you to bring revival to Ventura!"

What? How could I possibly do that? I was one person. But that was what I very clearly heard. I wasn't a general like we read about in our textbooks—I was only a few years removed from my Holy Spirit baptism and hadn't even finished seminary yet! Of course, the books I was reading discussed how many people God worked through weren't in the least bit qualified, yet He used them, some very effectively. In the Bible, God used Gideon, three Hebrew slave boys, Shadrach, Meshach, Abednego, and even a donkey. Before being called by Jesus, Peter's largest concern was his fishing business—look how God used him.

I told my wife what I had heard. Neither of us had a clue how to even start with such a massive assignment. Through my deliverance classes, I knew I had to pray and learn and know Scripture to be effective in deliverance ministry. I had witnessed that young pastor call upon the Holy Spirit for wisdom and guidance at the beginning of my deliverance session. The problem was I hadn't quite learned to generalize those deliverance spiritual resources into other areas of my spiritual life. I was convinced I had learned nothing that would help me meet the challenges of birthing a revival.

Joaquin was a major help. First off, he recommended a book by Bill Johnson: *When Heaven Invades Earth*. This book blew the lid off of what I knew to be possible. Pastor Bill talked about his hunger for more of God and to see revival come to Bethel Church in Redding. He talked about a power encounter so strong he didn't know if he would survive it. His book taught Paula and me that we had spiritual authority that we never had a clue we possessed.

We also read *Good Morning, Holy Spirit* by Benny Hinn. His Holy Spirit encounter was so much like mine it made me jealous, because his lasted for nine months versus only twenty-eight days for me. Joaquin sent us tapes by Dr. Heidi Baker and Jill Austin. We began to attend conferences featuring anointed men and women who walked in miracles. Most importantly, we began to make regular trips to Redding.

Over the next few months, we learned parenting a revival wasn't so much a conscious undertaking, requiring hard work and effort, as it was souls seeking His presence. When we decided to get out of His way, seek His guidance, and "just say yes" (Just Say Yes became the name of our ministry), He would begin to use us for His purposes. We weren't the parents, He was, and it would only be done by partnering with His Spirit. We didn't know what we were doing or how to do it, but of course, He did.

We began to pray for His gifts and to seek His guidance in all things. This strategy worked, but not without some serious bumps and bruises along the way.

CROSSING THE CHICKEN LINE

I remember the day Paula and I took a gamble and played a Dr. Heidi Baker tape for our elders at one of our board meetings. Dr. Heidi Baker is a completely sold-out lover of Jesus, and to say she is an unconventional speaker is a gross understatement. She is awesome and presents a pure, raw example of someone totally free of any fear of man. Heidi exudes the presence of God like no other I've met.

Heidi was being typical Heidi as she manifested Holy Spirit throughout the recording, with noises and utterings that sound totally off the charts if you're expecting a polished biblical scholar and not someone completely abandoned to Holy Spirit, as she is. If you are uninitiated to the moves of the Holy Spirit and those who allow Him to manifest through them, you will not know what to make of someone like Dr. Heidi Baker. She manifests the Holy Spirit like no one else, and to witness it is to be exposed to the raw presence of God. As Jesus said in Matthew 13:9, "He who has ears to hear, let him hear!"

We were laughed at and openly ridiculed as spiritual infants who had no idea of what real Christianity was about. We weren't asked to resign, but our standing amongst our fellow elders was definitely diminished.

We still had so much to learn. People we considered more spiritually advanced than us weren't necessarily as advanced in the things of the Spirit as we might have thought. The Holy Spirit was leading us into a world of worship and fellowship others were not willing to pursue. It was too radical and off the beaten path. It was not known, and it was frightening to most to leave the safe confines of the well-known. The familiar and acceptable was cozy and safe, where there was no chance of being an outlier if you stayed in the middle of the pack.

What we were pursuing was radical to most mainstream Christians, but we had lived most of our adult lives as radicals. We had been extreme political radicals back in the day. Now, we were rapidly becoming extreme spiritual radicals for Christ, and we loved it. However, after that elder meeting, we kept a low profile for quite a while. As a matter of fact, we wanted to leave that church, but Father wouldn't let us. He was very clear; we were to stay. Our mission was not over yet.

Our question was how we were to partner with Father God in bringing revival to a community when the church we were in covenant with was totally rejecting the idea? We tried to introduce our colleagues to different writings. We tried to convince them to come to conferences with us, to no avail. The outright rejection continued unabated.

Then, I got a revelation. If I could not start the fires of revival inside my church, then I needed to find fresh kindling outside my church. But how would we do that without breaking covenant? The Lord forbade us to leave. We were expressly directed to stay in fellowship. How could we accomplish what God wanted without going against the wishes of our leaders? I had already been reprimanded for taking a group from our church to see Kim Clement, a well-known prophet. I didn't believe in disobedience, so there had to be another way.

We had been leading a home group for some time. Our pastor carefully prepared the order of each meeting in every home, including any teachings. As time went on, he became less diligent about preparing the agenda for each bi-weekly meeting; I believe the task became too ponderous for him. With no new teachings,

Paula and I began filling in the gaps with past teachings and old instructions.

The thought occurred to us to start introducing new reading material to our group of eight to ten people. We began reading and discussing books on healing, spiritual warfare, and revival. We would research Bible references to validate what we were reading, and members could also suggest and share reading material. Excitement and new life began to infuse the group as we started to pray for spiritual gifts and then to pray for each other.

What happened next was phenomenal! We began to see people get healed almost every meeting. Joaquin was visiting when Karen, one of our members, brought her deaf mother to the meeting. The lady could only hear with hearing aids. Joaquin led us in a healing prayer, and when we were done, he asked her to remove her hearing aids. He began to test her hearing by speaking at the same volume as he moved further and further away from her. To our delight and her amazement, she could hear just as well from across the room as she could when he was right next to her without her hearing devices.

The more we prayed for God's presence, the more He showed up in signs and wonders. God planted a seed in our home and in the hearts of those friends who attended our little group. His intention was clear—plant the seed in good soil where it would meet little resistance, and watch it grow and spread.

The atmosphere in our little church was electric with anticipation. The members of our home group who also attended our church were waiting for the Spirit to break forth during one of our meetings. It finally happened one Sunday service when Julie, a member of our home group, began laughing during worship. She was sitting on the carpet in the back of the sanctuary by herself. Immediately, I recognized her laugh was no ordinary laughter. I decided to take a risk and join her on the floor. As I got up from my normal front-row seat, I fully expected our pastor to stop me. He was a stern man who didn't tolerate a lot of outward demonstration of emotion during service. He once chastised us for saying "Come on" and "That's good" too many times during his preaching. His exact words from the pulpit, in a very sarcastic tone were, "Come on, come on, come, on! I don't need your encouragement!" That was during our first few weeks of attending the church. It set an undeniable tone for the deportment he expected from his attendees.

If you've ever experienced genuine holy laughter, you know it's contagious. Holy laughter is when the Holy Spirit invades your consciousness and brings you such joy at His presence you can't help but get happy. I sat down next to Julie and immediately felt His presence all over her. At this writing it's been two decades since that day and I can still feel the electricity of His presence coursing through my body as if it were yesterday.

I began to laugh as well. Soon I was laughing uncontrollably with her. Tears were streaming down our faces. One by one, members of the congregation began to turn to see what was happening. They looked puzzled at first, but slowly the slightest signs of smiles began cracking through their once placid facial expressions. Of course, the members of our group knew exactly what was happening. Most of them joined in to some degree—some wholeheartedly, while others held back just a little.

We were all waiting for the pastor's booming voice to demand to know why those people were inappropriately disrupting service, but it never came. I didn't know what to make of it, other than it was a small miracle (if there is such a thing as a small miracle). Perhaps he was more tolerant because it was worship and not during his sermon, or maybe it was because he felt it too. I don't know, but I do know that day marked a turning point in the inevitable revival to come.

CHAPTER 20

A TASTE OF REVIVAL

Prayer for healing became more and more prevalent in our church. It wasn't part of our services yet, but no one seemed to mind because there was a lot of prayer happening on the periphery, God was moving, and people were getting healed. People were escaping their wheelchairs, blindness was fleeing, and so was deafness. It was great. People in our little church were beginning to see and believe God was truly alive, was healing His people today, and loved them unconditionally.

But, of course, when the devil sees people getting free, he tries to derail what God is doing. The enemy struck. He had to do something to divert this fledgling move of God. Some issues arose and our senior pastor had to resign. This was a blow to the congregation because most of us were there because of this man's teaching. He was rather stern but knew his Bible and was an excellent teacher. He also had a passion for Israel and taught us to have a passion for the Jewish people and Israel as well.

I will not go into detail, but it was a rough season. The elders chose not to reveal all the details to our congregation to protect innocent people, which in some ways made things worse. People didn't understand what was happening. Some thought the elders were staging a coup; others were just confused and wanted answers. The enemy had effectively, though temporarily, averted our attention to this issue.

The elders immediately went into search mode to find our next pastor. We executed a nationwide search yielding many candidates, but none fitted any of the characteristics we all could agree on. We decided to look internally. The two leading candidates were myself and another senior elder. The choices were very interesting. On the one hand there was me, an inexperienced church leader on fire for God and revival, and on the other hand was a very good guy who was in love with Jesus and had a huge heart for the Ventura Avenue Community.

Ventura is a civic diamond perfectly situated between Los Angeles and Santa Barbara. In 2005-06 it was a diverse community made up of very expensive homes sprawled along the Pacific shore, with homes just as elegant nestled in the Ventura Hills, and thriving middle-class neighborhoods with sprawling lawns and neatly tended homes dotted throughout the city. Then, there was the Ventura Avenue section of town. "The Ave," as it was (and still is) called, stretched from the Hills all the way down to the beach. The upper section nearest the Hills and the bottom section by the beach were populated with nice, middle-class condos, shops, offices, and homes. The middle section of the Ave was a different story. This is where our church was located, right in the middle of Ventura Avenue. Gangs sold drugs up and down the Ave and surrounding areas, all the way down to the beach, with the Hell's Angels International headquarters just a few short blocks away. This middle section of the Ave stretched about fifteen blocks and was populated with impoverished to lower-middle-class housing on both sides of the street extending outwardly for two or three blocks in each direction.

Our old pastor told stories of the times he, his wife, and kids had to dive for cover from bullets whizzing through the parsonage as gang members and dealers settled their disputes with gun fire on the streets outside. Things were a little better by the time Paula and I joined the church, but it was still a pretty rough neighborhood. I remember our first Sunday there. We sat in the back pews, and though it was 11:00 AM Sunday morning, many of the folks sitting around us had just come off the streets. Despite their hard lives and the smell of the streets lingering on them, they would come in every Sunday morning praising God and looking for the "more" the good news offered. Their lifestyles did not fill the gaping holes in their souls. No matter how many drugs they consumed or how much they stole, cheated, drank, or sold their bodies to earn enough to survive until tomorrow, happiness and self-worth eluded them. They were on an endless spiral that led deeper into the abyss. The people of our community were desperate for the "real" gospel of Jesus Christ, and these people made up a sizable portion of our congregation.

The choice had to be made. Who was going to fill the vacated position of senior pastor? My associate and I both felt called to the post, though I must admit I was very aware of my lack of experience leading a church. I had years of experience leading organizations and businesses, but not a church. We knew leading a church would truly stretch us. Paula was not as sure as I was and quite frankly, had her doubts. I was far from confident but didn't want to see the church retreat from the burgeoning revival God was orchestrating. As God often does, He spoke to my wife first. It was difficult for her to break the news to me, but she is a brave woman.

One day she simply said, "I don't feel like you should take the senior pastor position!"

I had a great deal of difficulty accepting this declaration. She couldn't give me a rational reason. She just knew that she knew.

When God speaks prophetically to someone, often times the insight will come without an explanation from Him, just a deep knowing that what you are sensing is true. Just like when you are sitting in a jail cell and a voice tells you that you are getting out!

We were still learning the deeper ways of God (and quite honestly, still are), but I knew enough to know when my wife received these insights, I needed to listen. Three weeks or so later, through prayer and seeking Him on what should be done, I felt the same message. God seemed to say to me I was not to take the senior position. I felt Him saying He would be moving us soon, and the church had been through enough change and turmoil. We had almost split more than once and keeping our small church of roughly a hundred and twenty souls together had been a miracle under very trying circumstances. Only through God's wisdom and our obedience to His scriptural teaching and His lead did we survive the rifts that had arisen over a short but intense time. This small but significant church in the roughest section of Ventura could not survive more upheaval. The church needed stability, therefore Paula and I leaving a short while after taking the reins was not what the church needed. Funny, God knew exactly what He was doing whether I agreed or not. We stepped aside and our friend took the position. This may have happened anyway, but at least more controversy was avoided by our decision.

A HOUSE DIVIDED

Things went well for a while, but soon our leadership grew divided as to how we should meet the needs of our community and address the despair and desperation our neighbors faced daily. Some advocated the church provide more programs to feed, clothe, and educate. Their argument was that basic needs had to be addressed, or we would fail our community. Paula and I agreed these programs were good and would please God, but we also recognized the enormity of the need. Our stance was the churches had been providing food, clothing, and recreational programs for years in our community with very little to show for it, and besides, our small church had limited resources. None of the senior leaders were accepting any salary from the church at all. As a matter of fact, we were pouring more money into the church than most. Our senior pastor was extremely generous and was pouring in thousands a month to keep things going. Any programs we initiated could not be sustained with the majority of our resources coming from our pastor's heartfelt generosity. The most damaging thing to our community would be to start programs and have to discontinue them. People in need are used to well-intentioned Christians and secular people coming into their communities with handouts and then leaving as suddenly as they had come. We needed these programs, but we needed more than just programs. We needed the presence of God empowering all we did to see any lasting change.

My wife and I felt the only viable course of action was to continuously seek the presence of God. Surrendering to the will of the Lord had radically changed my life and the lives of my family. We had witnessed the impossible become possible too many times. Programs were good and right, but room had to be made for the leading of God's Holy Spirit. As my son Joaquin likes to say, "We are always looking for something good to do for God and asking God to bless it, when what we should be doing is looking for what God is already blessing and start partnering with Him to do that!"

It's true we were new to church life, but I had been raised in the church and had partnered with our pastor and leadership in our rather large church in DC on many programs as a kid. Though we kept very busy and were doing a lot of good things for our community, I never saw much fruit from our efforts. I never personally witnessed anyone come to the Lord through our programs and offerings. I rarely witnessed any salvations, though I'm sure there were more here and there during church service I didn't see. In other words, there was a lot of work that made us feel good about ourselves, but very little kingdom advancement resulting from that work. The people we were attempting to help seemed to be pretty much unchanged by our interventions, and to be honest I don't know how you'd help someone get to a place you are not in yourself. I can only help you navigate to where I am, and points beyond that are as much a mystery to me as they are to the person I'm trying to help.

It seems many churches are no different than other nonprofit, community-based organizations. They all work hard and have the best of intentions, but many have limited impact in terms of long term change in the lives of the individuals and communities they serve. I'm not saying they have no impact at all; they do. Many have benefitted from the efforts of sincere believers and secular volunteers that serve and sacrifice for the needy, but there is so much more we can achieve when we partner with God.

The Welsh Revival and the Azusa Street Revival in Los Angeles that took place in the early 20th century sparked major movements that are still running strongly today in those countries and others. So much of the church either doesn't believe those events truly originated from God, or they look at them as isolated incidents that a "normal" Christian group couldn't possibly replicate. My question was and still is, "Why not?"

During the Welsh Revival, roughly 150,000 new converts filled the local churches (an amazing number for such a small country). Five years later, 82.5% of that number remained. Many of the missing 17.5% moved to Canada, the US, and Australia due to extreme hardships in Wales. Some historians believe that as many as 250,000 people were actually born again from 1904 to 1905, but not all joined established churches.

Most taverns in the country went bankrupt. Crime was cut in half, resulting in many police forces cutting half their staff. Jails and prisons closed. Production in the coal mines slowed down because the miners quit cursing. As a result, the horses they used to move the coal couldn't understand the miners' orders because they were so used to the miners using foul language. In one police precinct, the main function of the officers was to provide singing quartets during the church meetings every night. They had nothing better to do. The courts literally, on many days, had no cases to try.

A Bible student named Evan Roberts[1] is credited as the father of the Welsh Revival. He went from being a virtually unknown person to the most talked-about man in his country in two weeks! Why Evan Roberts? I believe God chose him because he was willing to submit his own agenda to follow God's. Roberts was known for this simple prayer: "Bend me, God."

In the spring of 1906, William Seymour, an African American pastor, and a small group of believers began to hold meetings at a modest home on Bonnie Brae Street in Los Angeles. Seymour, a pastor-teacher, blind in one eye from smallpox, began by teaching from Acts 2 in the Bible. He taught on the coming of the Holy Spirit and the baptism of the hundred and twenty who experienced the outpouring of God's Spirit. As a result, people began to experience the presence of God and received their own Holy Spirit baptisms.

In a few months, the meetings grew so large the neighbors complained and called the police. Seymour and his followers were forced to move to an old barn on Azusa Street.[2] There the meetings grew to capacity with over thirteen hundred people attending each meeting. Thousands experienced God and were filled with the Holy

Spirit. Still more thousands were healed—so many, in fact, that it is reported the top floor of the building was filled with crutches and canes discarded by those healed during the meetings held at Azusa Street.

Countless other miracles occurred. The fire department responded more than once to reports of the building being on fire, only to find the flames appearing above the building were a supernatural phenomenon that blew the minds of onlookers. It was fire from heaven, God's glory manifested in heavenly fire swarming above the building. Other written eyewitness accounts tell of glory clouds from God forming inside the building so thick people couldn't see one another. People who were just children during those events speak of trying to capture the substance of the clouds in jars to take home, only to discover that whatever the substance was dissipated before very long.

In a documentary narrated by Carriesno Shackles, we learned there were roughly a dozen major denominations formed out of the Azusa Street Revival. According to Shackles, an estimated 600 million Christians can trace their spiritual roots to Azusa Street. 600 million!

Revival brings about massive change mere programs cannot. The members and leaders of our small community church wanted to see those we served enjoy lasting change. We wanted our community healed and free of crime, drugs, and dysfunction. We wanted to not only see children fed, but whole families freed from fear, poverty, despair, and oppression. In other words, we wanted revival. We had no problem with programs to meet immediate needs, but we knew the only lasting solution was for the presence of God to fall upon West Ventura. We wanted to see heaven come to earth. In Matthew 6, the Lord's Prayer states, "Thy kingdom come, Thy will be done on earth as it is in heaven." If Jesus would have us pray this, then it must be something obtainable. One of the greatest revivals in history had occurred in our own backyard not thirty miles away in LA a mere hundred years earlier. Why couldn't God do it again with human partners willing to lay down everything to partner with Him in seeing "heaven come to earth"?

The issue of how to best serve our neighborhood seemed to reach an impasse. Paula and I continued to serve the church and follow the lead of our senior leader, but the fire in our hearts for revival never dissipated. We all finally agreed upon a course of action including both programs and the desire for revival. We would vigorously seek the Lord while continuing to serve West Ventura and the Ave with as many programs as we could handle.

We continued our weekend food and clothing distribution programs, our work with neighborhood children, and limited transportation back and forth to the church and other helpful locations. We also continued to operate our men's home, The King's House, located on the church grounds. The home provided shelter, life skills counseling, spiritual and pastoral counseling, and care to neighborhood men struggling with homelessness, addictions, and other life challenges. I taught free taekwondo classes to neighborhood kids in the church dining hall and at a local Boy's and Girl's Club with the help of my son, volunteers from my school, and The King's House.

In addition, we constantly sought the Lord through specific prayer and supplication. Our home group continued to meet bi-monthly and to grow in number. We walked the community while praying for revival and renewal, specifically targeting locations known for criminal and drug activity. We taught willing volunteers how to go out into the streets and find "treasures"—individuals the Holy Spirit would identify through prayer He wanted us to minister to before we ever left the building or ever saw them. A pastor named Kevin Dedmon developed this ministry technique, called "Supernatural Treasure Hunts." Years later we had the privilege of working with Kevin at Bethel Church in Redding, California, and became close friends. We prophesied over people and saw God save and heal countless afflictions on the streets of West Ventura through this technique.

We started a small school of ministry that became a passion for our senior leader and other leaders in the church.We invited well known revivalists to speak and brought teams from Bethel Church in Redding and other places. We also began to host a quarterly revival conference at our church and our sister church in Ventura called Horizon, which was originally founded by Aimee Semple McPherson. Many well-known revivalists came and preached the gospel, prayed for salvation, and released God's healing over all in attendance. As word grew about these conferences, people began to come in from LA and Santa Barbara to witness this growing move of God.

Matthew 6:33 instructs us to seek first the kingdom of God and His righteousness. That command seems pretty simple and straightforward, but how does one do that? We were discovering how.

A couple of years earlier, I'd enrolled part-time in The King's University and Seminary (called The King's College and Seminary back then). One evening while studying the Scriptures, I read Matthew 6:33, and though I'd read it many times, it struck me quite differently this time around. Here's the full verse from the New King James version: "But seek first the kingdom of God and His righteousness, and all these things shall be added to you."

Just as I read the last word of that verse, I looked up from the kitchen table where I was sitting and saw a very heavy collegiate dictionary, which my family had given me as a birthday present during grad school for my MBA, literally fly off of our bookcase in our family room and land with a tremendous thud on the carpeted floor. Our kitchen flowed two steps down into the family room, and my view was completely unobstructed.

"Okay God, I get it!" I said. Matthew 6:33 was to be my bedrock verse, the verse I was to operate from the rest of my life. Many verses in the Bible have impacted me in the years following in so many ways, but ever since that evening, Matthew 6:33 has remained my go-to verse and my foundation. You should read this passage yourself and let the Holy Spirit reveal to you its full meaning. Just before Matthew 6:33, in verses 25 through 32, Jesus admonishes us to not worry about our daily needs being met, but to make seeking God our highest priority and everything we worry about will be provided to us. Following these simple instructions requires us to grow both in faith and trust. Without these two elements, one cannot persistently and successfully pursue God, because the world will lure you into distraction. To me, it seemed pretty simple—I was to go after the "real God." I had met Him on a mountaintop, and now I was to seek Him to know Him in all His righteousness.

As a result of all this, we started to see God slowly transform our community. To our delight, people started investing in the area, buying and refurbishing houses, and bringing new upscale businesses to either end of the Ave. These businesses and new homes attracted folks in higher income brackets, stimulating the economy of the area. The Ventura Police Department reported a sharp decrease in crime on the Ave as well.

I'm not trying to take any credit for this turnaround—glory goes to God for it all. But partnering with God in what He wants to do is infinitely more powerful and effective than doing what we think is best. This is true in any situation, from making a change in your own life to transforming a community. What we've seen God do through revival throughout history far trumps what can be done through any programs conceived by mankind alone.

Before God started transforming our church, He began to move magnificently amongst our members. Miracles began to breakout on a regular basis. Our members and visitors to our conferences experienced God's goodness in spectacular ways. We saw blindness healed, deaf ears open, and countless diseases vanquished! People began to get free from addictions and very importantly, poverty. The spirits of poverty and despair were prevalent in our community, as you can well imagine. Through seeing others get healed and prosper in their finances and other areas, people began to realize it could happen for them as well. Our friends and neighbors started to understand God isn't good to just a few—He is good to all who accept Him and believe He wants to be good to them, too. They began to understand the riches of the kingdom are there for everyone, including them. People began to get new jobs, return to school, and grow in confidence in a brighter future.

You could see and feel the transformation amongst our church members, and, as confidence grew and attitudes began to shift, the church started to attract other like-minded folks. People who were healthy in mind and spirit, and who carried an expectation of good fortune in their lives, began to show up regularly. The transformation was underway, and it was all due to saying yes to Jesus.

As I mentioned earlier, Paula and I were candidates for the senior pastor position until the Lord told us a resounding "No!" He was clear. We would be leaving soon. My wife and I were obedient to the word we received from the Lord and continued to follow His lead and His plans for revival in the city. While witnessing the Lord do amazing things with our fellow believers, we watched and waited for signs that He was about to bring about another major shift in our lives.

It took about three years before the awaited shift finally happened. It was not until early 2010 when it became very clear our departure from the life we had built in Southern California was imminent. Situations we had been somewhat comfortable in for years were becoming increasingly more difficult. The surgery center where Paula held a supervisory position was sold to a company that brought in difficult and cumbersome policies and procedures. Plus, she no longer had direct access to the doctor who owned the surgery center and the practice. He was still there, but the buck no longer stopped with him. Paula had worked with this doctor for years and had helped build a large and very successful business. She was used to very nice bonuses at the end of each year along with a fair amount of autonomy to supervise her nurses and staff in order to keep things running smoothly, which they very much did. Under this new corporate structure, all that began to change and became very uncomfortable for her. The grace was lifting. After several difficult months, she decided to leave the job and the people she had held dear for many years. Her next position was as a nurse evaluator with the State of California Department of Health Services.

Meanwhile, the economic downturn in the last part of the decade was drastically affecting my martial arts school and supply business. Student enrollment dropped from over two hundred to less than a hundred and thirty students. Our revenue from supply sales was meager as well. My classes at Ventura College remained strong, but my salary there was not predicated on the number of students in each class, though I'd always enjoyed a steady influx of students into Premier Martial Arts from the college. Students could only take my martial arts and self-defense class at the college for four semesters each, so when they were maxed out at the college, they would simply cross Telephone Road and enroll in Premier if they wished to continue their training. However, the college had been suffering cutbacks in every department since 2007. My martial arts class and personal safety courses were very popular. Each usually had a waiting list to get into, so the dean was reluctant to pull either of them, but I knew if the cuts continued to increase my turn would come. The dean was getting down to essential courses that, under contract with local government agencies, he couldn't cut, like several criminal justice courses, required physical education classes, athletic department courses and teams, and classes that had more tenure than mine. Again, the grace was slowly lifting.

Things at the church appeared to be routine; however, the denominational higher-ups at our sister church across town had ordered them to stop partnering with us in this local revival movement. Despite the transformations we were witnessing in our congregations and communities, they didn't like the strong affiliation we had with Bethel Church in Redding, California. They felt like Horizon was under too much outside influence. We all played Bethel music during worship and enjoyed a constant flow of pastors and evangelists visiting and speaking at our two churches. When the senior pastor at our sister church didn't move fast enough to cut ties with us and Bethel, he and his wife were suddenly and very unceremoniously fired from both their senior pastor positions and as the head of their church-based Christian school. This had a very sobering effect on everyone at our little church as well. It was a great lesson on how movements of God can be quelled by the vanity of men. People were growing and being freed from all sorts of bondages in their lives, but that didn't matter as much as keeping control and adherence to policy. I'm not saying policies are bad in themselves—we need them. But we also need to be in the business of setting people free and getting them into the presence of God over adhering to controlling policies. Yielding to the leading of the Holy Spirit needs to trump legalism.

Our duties and positions at Avenue Community Church continued unchanged; however, I was getting fewer opportunities to preach and share the message of revival. It was the senior pastor's responsibility to preach on Sundays, of course. Associates rarely preach in small churches unless the senior is away or unavailable. However, I used to be allowed to preach every few weeks and looked forward to the opportunity each time. The reduction in pulpit time meant fewer opportunities to share our passion for revival. It was okay, we had dropped out of consideration for the senior position out of obedience and were committed to serve the vision of our friend and current leader; however, again, we could feel grace lifting. We no longer felt comfortable in our jobs, in our church, or even in most of our relationships. Almost, without noticing it, something had shifted. We didn't necessarily know it at the time, but God was creating an atmosphere around us so that when He gave the command to go, we would go with little or no hesitation, like an arrow under the tension of a strong archer's drawn bow released to find its target.

CHAPTER 21

A NEW DAWN

By mid 2010, we felt the time for the major change the Lord had told us would come was drawing near. Jahi was married and living in Cyprus. He and Kes were helping to lead a missionary training school for Gateways Beyond International and were taking teams to the nations, and Joaquin was working at Bethel Church running the Healing Rooms, as well as preaching all over the world.

We knew we were supposed to move but didn't know where. We had invitations to join friends in Mexico at their missionary post and school of ministry, as well as an invitation to join Gateways Beyond at one of their international bases. And the idea of joining the revival in Northern California at Bethel Church was a constant draw.

As Paula and I prayed and sought the Lord for direction for our next assignment from Him, an idea began to form. We felt drawn to the mission field. The idea of serving our friends the Taylors in Mexico for part of the year and Gateways in Cyprus another part of the year excited us. We felt that if the Lord blessed us and we were smart financially, we could keep a home in the States we'd rent out while we were gone and then spend the rest of the year serving the vision of these amazing ministries for four to five months at a time.

By now, Paula had been working for the State of California a few years. She was nearing the minimal time on the job allowing her to retire with some benefits, but the deciding factor came when the dean of our department at the college visited my martial arts school. Though my school was right across the Avenue from the college, he had never visited me at my office at Premier, and by the look of regret on his face, I could see he was not bringing good news. The faculty cuts had finally reached me. He didn't have to say it. Without a word, I knew it was true. I had been expecting this day for over a year. God was speaking clearly, and the time to make a break from our current lives and move on had come.

I interrupted him before he got to the point. I wanted to spare him the chore of having to give me bad news, so I told him I had decided to resign my teaching position. The look on his face was pure relief. He admitted letting me go was not something he wanted, but he was down to bare bones and had been ordered to cut another ten percent from his annual budget, for a total of forty percent in the last four years.

I was very apprehensive about the future, but at the same time felt somewhat liberated. Now was the time to put the plan into action. It seemed like a very doable plan. We decided that since Joaquin was getting married in the spring and housing was much more affordable in Redding than in Southern California, we would move there and establish a home base. And, of course, Bethel was located there. What a bonus. It seemed like a win-win; we'd help with the wedding, be near our son and his new bride, Renée, worship and fellowship at Bethel when we were not on the mission field, and have a great home base. It seemed perfect.

But how many times does God dangle a dazzling idea in front of you just to get you moving in a certain direction? The answer is quite often, if you are one who operates out of radical obedience to Him. Sometimes I picture myself as a kid with my natural father, Jay, dangling something shiny and glittery in front of me to get me to come to him. I would come, and instead of getting the much-sought after and desirable dangling thing, Dad would snatch me up in his arms and shower me with love and hugs. Sometimes, a little training and equipping comes before the hugs and affection. The equipping may mean going through a challenging situation that ultimately prepares you to do the one thing God wants you to do. The hugs may come later, but the love is always there.

I don't think we were ready to go into the mission field at that point in our growth and development, though we certainly thought we were. I had been on just a few short-term ministry trips, and Paula had made several trips to Cyprus, but we had never faced the true rigors of the mission field. We knew several outstanding souls who regularly invited us to join them either short-term or as permanent members of their teams, but we didn't have nearly enough experience.

I'm not speaking about physical toughness here, but the kind of spiritual grounding it takes to face the trials ahead. In developing countries (which is where we were headed), people don't have a plan B. There is no health insurance, no rapid transit, or supermarkets. Healthcare of any kind is minimal at best, and nutrition is basic and often lacking while disease can be rampant. When people have nothing and are facing death or starvation, your physical skills can only go so far. When people have few options, people need to hear the gospel and they need miracles, and miracles were something we had not learned to consistently operate in yet.

We resigned our positions at the church, Paula got a transfer at her State job to a Northern California branch, and we sold Premier in early 2011. We made our way to Redding, California, by May. Joaquin and Renée were married in June, and soon after we wrapped up the sale of our SoCal home and settled into life in Redding.

The plan we had set out to implement seemed to be working just fine—until it wasn't. We ran into some serious financial issues, and had to go back to work in secular jobs full-time. Paula's retirement date from her State job kept being extended due to technicalities. We found ourselves getting stuck in a rut we didn't expect and certainly didn't want. What we didn't realize was God had a plan for us that was a little different than what we thought.

We soon found ourselves on an adventure we could not have imagined. Anyone who thinks life in ministry is boring is not well informed—especially not a life in radical revival ministry.

For the first six months after we permanently settled into our little rental house, I wasn't working. I filled my time with volunteering at Bethel and deep-diving into the Word and His presence daily. I spent hours reading the Scriptures and seeking God through worship and prayer. During this time, I learned how much I didn't know. The Scripture began to reveal its secrets to me. It was like peeling off layers of an onion but the peeling away never seemed to diminish its size. Instead, the more I peeled the more I realized was there. To this day I know I will never plumb the depths of God's Word. It's easy to see how a person could spend their entire lives studying just one book of the Holy Bible, let alone its entirety. I was just beginning to know things. Often times I found I didn't need to pray about something; I just seemed to know what to do, what direction to go, or what was right to do or not do. This is called receiving a "word of wisdom" (see 1 Corinthians 12:4-11).

I loved volunteering in the Healing Rooms at Bethel, overseen by Joaquin, and at a ministry named Firestarters, founded by Kevin Dedmon, a pastor on staff at the church. I had worked in the Healing Rooms on the occasions when I was visiting from SoCal and had also done some volunteer work at the Healing Rooms in Ventura. I looked forward to coming every Saturday, especially after I began to witness some spectacular miracles of healing after praying for people. On my visits, I had simply shadowed Joaquin, but now that I was there permanently, I was assigned to a team. After a few months I became a team leader and began seeing mind-boggling moves of God.

Speaking of miracles, let me backtrack a bit. Right after packing up and selling our home in Camarillo and returning to Redding in August of 2011, I witnessed a manifestation of God's glory. We were in an evening service and Pastor Bill Johnson was giving the word, when gradually this dust began to accumulate in the air. It started in one section of the sanctuary and slowly moved until it covered everything, including the stage. It seemed to grow in thickness as the worshippers became more aware of it. As if in direct response to our excitement, it began to swirl and almost dance all around us. It was golden in color and consisted of very small flake-like material that would cling to your clothing and skin, then dissolve into nothingness! I am so thankful I had the presence of mind to capture some of the flakes in a few photos.

As amazing as that was, what was even more fascinating was Pastor Bill's reaction. To my amazement, he continued to preach. I wondered if he even noticed this miracle unfolding right before his very eyes. He soon stopped and acknowledged God's presence, but stated that though we should be awed by this manifestation, we shouldn't be surprised when God shows up amongst His people. As true believers, we need to know He is real and will be amongst us sometimes in very real physical ways. This same phenomenon repeated, just as spectacularly, a couple of months later in early October. A friend of mine, Jim, who owns a heating and air business, told me what we all witnessed would be impossible to fake. The way the gold dust was behaving and undulating could not be created by air being pumped through ventilation systems or any other way. He said the dust looked like it was alive and was moving under its own power. From what I witnessed, Jim's assessment was right-on.

Now, I was positive we had made the right move by coming to Redding and to Bethel Church. As I stated earlier, the moment I moved to Redding, I enrolled in a class at Bethel called Firestarters, created by Kevin Dedmon. Our spiritual son, Eddie, had insisted I enroll. He was adamant, and I thought if he was that insistent, I should at least check it out. I was a little skeptical and, I have to admit, not very humble. The class was about activating and equipping believers to become on-fire revivalists. Hadn't Paula and I almost singlehandedly brought revival to Ventura? I mean, could this class really teach me anything?!

We arrived in Redding on a Friday near the end of May in 2011. By that Sunday, we were sitting in Firestarters. At first glance, the material seemed very elementary, and Paula and I exchanged glances with one another as if saying, "This is like Revival 101, a beginner's class!"

In a way, it was. The material was sort of aimed at rudimentary elements of establishing a revival culture. Many people need to start there to completely capture the spirit of revival. But what blew us away was the tangible presence of God we experienced every Sunday as the entire class of eighty to a hundred hungry believers pulled heaven to earth. The atmosphere was electric as the presence of God descended upon the room. The experience would make us giddy with heavenly joy at times and oddly sober at others. It was simultaneously invigorating and humbling.

I realized what I had experienced before coming to Bethel was just the tip of the iceberg. I was beginning to understand there was so much more to God than anyone could fathom. I knew this intellectually before, but this was experiential. Just as my mountaintop experience had taught me God can and will allow us to taste and see His goodness and the immense joy of His presence, what I was now experiencing was teaching me that we serve a multifaceted God who can manifest in so many different ways. God can reveal Himself magnificently as gold dust or as the most subtle of bodily sensations. He can make money appear from nowhere (as He did for us one morning when we were broke, and getting pretty desperate) or in a word of knowledge when He tells you something about another person you couldn't possibly know.

The acceleration in growth was heady stuff. Bethel, and especially Firestarters, had a saying that they spelled faith R-I-S-K. In other words, we had to take risks to grow and become the on-fire revivalists we all wanted to be. I saw people who had never given a prophetic word in their lives step to the front of the class and give someone a prophecy. Sometimes they got it right, and sometimes they didn't. However, everyone was applauded just as vigorously whether their prophetic word was accurate or not, just for having the courage to step up and take a risk. The funny thing was every time they stepped up they got better. We saw it time and again. Everyone appeared to improve over time, so by the time they graduated in twelve weeks, most were amazingly accurate.

It was the same for praying for the sick. We were amazed at the number of miracles we witnessed every week in Firestarters, the Healing Rooms, where I eventually became a pastor, and in the church as a whole!

I learned that, 1) everyone is empowered to operate in the gifts of the Spirit, and 2) there is effective, operational power in going after God corporately.

As the months and years passed, I began to see revival from the heavenly perspective of a true apostolic leader and teacher, Pastor Bill Johnson. I encourage anyone reading these words to experience the work and teachings of Bill Johnson for themselves. The truth of his teachings, his perspective on the true nature of God, and how we can be accessing heaven here on earth now is self-evident.

A NEW TEST

Eventually, we finally found some balance in our lives. Paula found a job in a surgery center where she was highly appreciated and valued by her co-workers and supervisors alike, and I was working for an international criminal justice organization (God does have a sense of humor) where I had the opportunity to help many dear souls lost on the wrong side of the criminal justice system find their true purpose in life again. We had challenging jobs in the secular world, jobs that often challenged us to keep our focus on Jesus and not what the world dictated as correct, but we were managing it all rather well.

Then came dire news. I was diagnosed with prostate cancer in November of 2015. I had been feeling very sluggish for weeks, finding it hard to stay awake at work even with adequate sleep the night before. Several times I jerked awake in the middle of the afternoon at my desk, not realizing that I'd ever fallen asleep. I was the program's director so, fortunately, I had my own office and no one noticed, but it was highly unusual for me. After running some tests and examining my prostate, my urologist called in late November to inform us that it was indeed cancer.

Though we were determined to put our trust and faith in the Lord and to believe in Him for a healing, that Thanksgiving was not the most joyous one we'd ever had. I felt as if I'd been roundhouse kicked in the gut by a fourth-degree black belt (a sensation I was, unfortunately, very familiar with). It wasn't the first time my faith had been challenged by my worldly circumstances. I admit it was difficult at times to keep my focus on the Lord and His promises. Memories of friends and family who had succumbed to this disease kept swirling around in my head, battling against the truth of God's goodness. By now I had witnessed God do so many fantastic things: tumors expelled into a trash can after we'd prayed for a lady, a kid's blind eye fully restored in Ecuador, people getting up from wheelchairs after years of bondage to their devices, and so many deaf ears healed I'd lost count. Still, the lies of Satan kept oppressing my thoughts and memories; "You won't get healed. You're a fool to think this will happen for you. Your past has finally caught up to you." It was a battle for my mind and soul, not just my body.

Soon after Thanksgiving, we went into warfare mode. Cancer had delivered a devastating punch, but we were not going to just lie down and take it. We decided to punch back. We sought prayer from trusted family members and friends, and from the Bethel Healing rooms. We began doing research on every aspect of this disease and on every treatment option available. We had been told the tumor was of the slow-growing variety, but that we should not wait more than six to eight weeks before seeking treatment. After a few weeks of prayer, more tests and exams, the results showed no signs of the cancer resolving.

Despite the protestations of my urologist (who wanted to perform surgery to remove my prostate), we decided to enroll in a proton radiation program at Loma Linda University Hospital in Loma Linda, California. The treatment regimen was no picnic, but the side effects promised were much less severe than surgery and other more traditional programs promised, and the success rate (getting all of the tumorous cancer cells) was about the same. The downside to Loma Linda's program was I would be away from home and family for about two and a half months. The forty-five treatments would be uncomfortable but safe, and I would retain the ability to be intimate with my wife.

After visiting the facilities in Southern California, we decided to proceed with the treatments. I took an extended leave from my job, rented a room in a lovely home from a very nice lady and her father, and began the proton radiation treatments and the battle for my life around February 1, 2016. I started the program with my trust in God still intact, but if I was totally honest, I'd have to admit I was a little angry with Him. How many miracles of healing had I seen by now? Hundreds! Including cancer! My constant question to Him was, "Why, God? Why don't You just heal me like so many others I've seen and heard about? Why do I have to go through all this?'

I'm being completely transparent here. I'm not proud of the attitude I carried back then, but it is also true. I didn't get it. I'm not sure I wanted to get it. I was anointed. I'd seen God move in miraculous ways. I was puffed up with my own importance, and I was ticked off! But mostly, I was just plain scared.

Throughout it all though, I kept the two-way communications open. I kept talking to God, but strangely, He wasn't answering. I couldn't blame Him since all I was mostly doing was whining. Until one day…

CHAPTER 22

UNCONDITIONAL LOVE

I was lying in my special capsule the technicians at the hospital make for each proton radiation patient. It's a plastic mold of your body, which you slip into before each treatment, placed in a cylindrical capsule (it looks like a huge half barrel) and loaded into what they called the gantry. It's mostly hidden from the patient's sight by false walls and ceilings, but the gantry is a huge three-story-tall apparatus housing the radiation device that rotates around the "passenger" while he is resting in the capsule (there were no women in the prostate cancer program, of course). Once in the capsule, a balloon is placed up the patient's rectum and then inflated with water. The whole excruciating, life-saving procedure takes about a half-hour.

By this time, thirteen to fourteen sessions into my forty-five-treatment protocol, I was feeling pretty sorry for myself. I had the whole "woe is me" victim mentality thing down to a tee. During this specific round of treatments, I was voicing my displeasure to God when I felt a spiritual backhand slap to the forehead. I know that doesn't sound very Christian, but it definitely beats what God did to the Israelites when Moses came off his mountaintop encounter with God to catch the people complaining and dancing around a golden cow, rebelling against Him. I count myself lucky with just a slap. "Thank You, Lord, for Your grace."

After He got my attention, these words came to me, "Stop whining! I am healing you but through medicine. You have seen My miraculous healing power, but so many who do not believe in Me have not. I want even those who will not come to Me for a healing (believer or not) to receive a healing, as well. Who do you think gave Dr. James Slater (My loyal servant) the inspiration to build this device you are in? You, and others I am revealing this knowledge to, will testify that I want all healed and that a medical healing is not to be dismissed. It is from Me as well!"

I think I lay in the machine a good two to three minutes after the treatment was over, too stunned to move. I probably would have been there all morning if the techs hadn't finally kicked me out to start preparing for the next patient.

Needless to say, I felt very small, petty, and quite corrected. I didn't complain to God, to myself, or anyone else for the remaining thirty plus treatments. As a matter of fact, my entire attitude and demeanor did a hundred-eighty-degree turn. I always knew, that I knew, that I knew I would be healed. After all, He was not done with me yet. But now, I knew why God was doing what He did. My treatment and cure had a purpose—one I planned to follow.

I finished the treatments and was released with a clean bill of health in mid-April of 2016. After spending a night in a seaside hotel in Pismo Beach with Paula to regain a small bit of my equilibrium, we headed straight back to Redding. As God would have it, my first week back we attended a conference for medical professionals promoted by Paul Manwaring called *Medicine Is Not a Second-Class Healing!*

Paul had been diagnosed with prostate cancer in the recent past and had to make a decision, like so many men have to do, on how to proceed. Paula and I met with Paul before deciding on our course of treatment. Paul had sought medical treatment for a cure after much prayer, as I had, and had come through healthy and healed. We were both very encouraged by his courage and his conviction that medicine is a totally acceptable choice for believers to make to find their way back to health. We discussed options and post-treatment life. Being a registered nurse himself, his advice was both sound and reassuring.

God's word to me to not disdain medical healing was total confirmation for Paul's position on the subject, and when I heard about what the title of his conference was, I knew it was exactly what God had spoken to me.

I was released from the hospital about forty-eight hours before Paul's conference, so, though still a little weak and dazed, I was able to attend. I was starved for fellowship with my clan. Plus, Joaquin was one of the conference speakers, so I insisted on going. As it turned out, I was very glad I did.

On the first day, I was sitting on the front row enjoying the program when I felt a tap on my shoulder. A couple sitting behind me noticed the tag on my key ring from the Loma Linda University Hospital Health and Fitness Center. They were physicians from Loma Linda Hospital and wanted to know if I was one as well. I told them I was not but had recently been released from there as a patient. When they discovered I was a pastor at Bethel, they asked me to pray for a friend from Dallas, Texas, attending the conference. I agreed.

Their friend was a believer but was having a little difficulty understanding how Jesus and miracles could play a part in his cardiology practice. The scientist in him could not reconcile how science and religion could merge. He saw them as separate things, like oil and water—he knew both existed but could not see them mixing.

As we talked, I realized a logical approach with this man of science was not the proper tack. I decided to bypass logic and speak directly to his spirit man, but I didn't get very far with that approach either. I asked permission to lay my hand on him and began to pray a simple prayer for the Holy Spirit to give him divine revelation on how much He wanted to partner with this doctor in healing his patients. The moment I placed my hand on his forehead and began to pray, the man began to violently shake and went down to the ground like he'd been shot with a high-powered rifle. He was down and out!

This all happened during a short break in the conference, and we just happened to be gathered near a doorway. When the Holy Spirit hit this man, he went down and partially blocked the doorway, making it difficult for the conference attendees to pass through. We couldn't move him. He was totally limp, dead weight. Onlookers tried to help him to his feet, but his legs wouldn't cooperate. He remained unsteady, wavering back and forth, even after regaining some control of his legs. He was clearly stunned and disoriented. The man looked around like he was just coming out of a drunken stupor (which, in a sense, he was) and asked, "What happened?"

I explained he had just encountered the Holy Spirit and God had heightened his spiritual awareness and sensitivity so radically because He so desperately wants him to know He is real. Personally, I was still feeling a little shaky as well, so instead of following up with more instruction to the Dallas doc myself, I asked some knowledgeable witnesses nearby to explain to our new friend exactly what (and Who) he was experiencing. As far as I'm aware, I've never seen him again, but I pray he grew in his walk with the Lord and is still being used mightily by God to bring supernatural healing through his practice!

It is no coincidence I was released from the treatment program just in time to attend Pastor Paul Manwaring's conference. In God's kingdom, there is no such a thing as coincidence. What we all experienced there went a long way in confirming what God had already taught me. God will heal His people in whatever way or means He chooses!

CHAPTER 23

BACK TO SERVICE

After returning home in April of 2016, I immediately dove back into church life and ministry. I resigned my position with the criminal justice organization I'd been working for, officially retiring. I was very grateful for the job and the benefits that came with it. Between their insurance and Medicare, I had paid just thirty-five dollars out of pocket for a treatment series costing well over one hundred thousand dollars. God is so good and faithful.

I've always had a military mentality. It helped me stay strong when I was going through some really rough times growing up. My plan was to join the military and make a career of it. In the military you know your assignment, your duty is clear, you know what you can do, and what you cannot. There are clear parameters and people there to make sure you follow the rules. The military represents authority and accountability. Though I never joined the United States military, you know my background with civilian military organizations and the Black Panther Party. Though not always achieving this goal, I've always had a heart to serve, to seek structure, and to live honorably in all I've done. I think that is partially why I thrived in and adapted so well to martial arts.

I've approached my Christian life the same way. I liken saying "yes" to Jesus and making Him the King of my life to joining His army. A Messianic rabbi prophet, who knew nothing of my history, once told me I was like a ninja or a special ops warrior penetrating the lines of the enemy, challenging and exposing lies and falsehoods.

Just like any good soldier, when God says move, we move! When God says stay, we stay. Sometimes the going and the staying are not easy. At times it's hard, but it's never boring. God had a mission for us that would include the entire family (including Eddie and his family). This mission would include the biggest move and challenge of our Christian lives, and it was coming soon.

After returning home from Loma Linda and retiring from full-time work, I threw myself into volunteer service at Bethel. I was on disability and still a little shaky from the radiation ordeal, but I was soon thrust into a challenge that would stretch and grow me like only God could.

The Firestarters ministry was going well, and I was welcomed back by the team with open arms. It felt so good to be back, and while it was probably a mistake, the team had me teach the very first Sunday I was back. I had a difficult time focusing and bringing much energy to the lesson, but it was just what I needed to shift my mind from Southern California and what I had just gone through.

As the weeks went by, I made steady progress. I felt my equilibrium slowly returning and was steadily regaining traction in my normal life, settling back into a familiar routine, minus working full-time.

Eddie had always been the de facto leader of Firestarters whenever Kevin was on the road preaching, which was fairly often. Kevin was in high demand, is an excellent speaker, and delivers the gospel like few can. But back in December right before we went to visit Loma Linda, Eddie had decided to focus his attention on his family of seven, including five girls, and work. He visited when he could, and we spoke frequently about the ministry, but he wasn't an active participant.

Upon my return, I found myself as the senior person on our leadership team—a task I embraced even though my head was still in a constant fog the first few weeks. Then, in June, another senior leader, Jason, announced he was going to take his family on an extended road trip for the summer. They had a beautiful motor home and traditionally took annual road trips so their kids could be exposed to different aspects of our beautiful country.

Secretly, I had been hoping this year would be different, that he would stay in Redding for some reason. About the same time, Kevin took an extended leave from his ministries at Bethel for personal reasons. This development came without much warning, but we all understood that sometimes we need to focus on ourselves and on our families.

I totally understood, but I was nervous about the health of the ministry without Eddie and Jason and now Kevin. However, I trusted God and knew being in this situation was no accident. God, in His infinite wisdom, knew I needed to gain confidence in my ability to manage an important ministry. With all three of these essential pastors out of the picture, it was up to me and the remaining leaders, Heather, Alexander, Tizita, and Darryll, to keep the fires burning hot and bright in one of Bethel's more catalytic ministries.

While this would have been enough of a challenge, that wasn't all. God had more challenges in store. Alexander and Tizita Logia announced they were leading a crusade through the Philippines that summer and knew they would be gone for several weeks but weren't quite sure just how long they would be away. It was an awesome opportunity, and I knew the world would be greatly blessed by the kingdom spirit they carried. Just as with Jason, we blessed them and sent them out to change the Asian Pacific.

With their departure, Heather, Darryll, and I were left to run a ministry consisting of about twenty-eight team members and approximately one-hundred enrolled students and guests. Darryll was, and is, an international speaker, and he and his wife Sondra are in-demand Sozo trainers (a powerful inner healing ministry). This meant he was away quite a bit (that's the reason Firestarters had a seven-member leadership team, because so many traveled the world for Christ).

You might think, "What's the big deal? Lots of people manage ministries and other operations much larger than this." The big deal was this ministry was embedded in Bethel Church, a church known for fantastic moves of God and for introducing believers to His supernatural nature and literally changing thousands of lives. It took senior leadership of the church weeks to conclude we could handle the responsibility and not lose Firestarters' catalytic fire. This ministry was, and is, known throughout the world as one that equips the saints to spread revival fire wherever they go. It is not as well-known as Bethel's School of Supernatural Ministry (BSSM), Bethel Music, or the Healing Rooms, but it still has a tremendous impact and reputation for producing believers who become serious influencers throughout the world. We had huge shoes to fill.

It all came together when Eddie returned to the ministry. Paula and I were scheduled to travel oversees that September and would be in Israel for two weeks. Not being sure when the Logia's would return and knowing Jason would not be back for a few weeks still, I was concerned about the minimal oversight this would leave for Firestarters during our absence. I made a heartfelt appeal to Eddie to return to the ministry. Fortunately, he had been missing us and was ready to come back. We were ecstatic. With Eddie and Heather (and the Holy Spirit, of course) at the helm every week, there was no doubt Firestarters would run smoothly.

Eddie returned in late May. Meanwhile, Jahi and Kes were contending for Israeli citizenship. As a Jew, it was Kes's right to make aliyah (the biblical return of all Jewish people to their traditional homeland). This wasn't just a biblical or traditional rite; it was a legal edict. Kes' parents, David and Emma Rudolph, and her brother Isaac, had been granted citizenship almost immediately after applying. The Rudolph's are well-known Messianic leaders throughout the world. For thirty plus years, they had traveled the planet, teaching the gospel to the Jewish people and anyone else who would listen, and equipping others to do the same. David and Emma and their family have established bases all over the world to promote the gospel of Y'shua Hamashiach (Jesus the Messiah).

Although non-Jewish Christians are welcomed in the land of our Lord, Jewish believers are feared and clandestinely blocked from gaining citizenship. There is no legal precedent for refusing aliyah to a Jewish person, so other reasons are usually conjured to block and thwart the process. David, Emma, and Isaac were approved, it is commonly believed, before the officials processing their application realized that they were *those* Rudolph's.

Jahi and Kes's application was held up for the most frivolous of reasons—requests for a rabbi's statement that her father was Jewish and her parents were married in a synagogue, requests for documents they had already submitted previously on multiple occasions, then requests for the originals of documents that were ancient and impossible to find. The process became so ridiculous they finally hired lawyers and fought the approval of their application all the way to the Supreme Court of Israel. During a break in the hearings, their lawyers told them if they persisted in their appeal they would likely be denied and forbidden from ever gaining citizenship if a negative decision was rendered. If they dropped their appeal, they would be able to bring the matter back before the courts at a later time. This option seemed the best. There was another case being heard that the lawyers felt had a better chance for a successful outcome. If this case was successful, it would set a favorable precedent for the Evans' case at a later time. After thinking this over in the few minutes they had in the outer halls of the court, they decided to drop the appeal.

Next came a bombshell. After informing the court of their decision to drop the appeal, the court gave its instructions before dismissing them. They ordered the Evans' to leave the country by July 1, 2016, effectively giving them thirty days to unravel three and a half years of life in Israel. They had to give up their home, sell or dispose of their furniture and all their possessions, abandon their work, and take the kids out of school. The kids spoke English well but were not proficient writers of the language.

With just thirty days to purchase tickets to the US, they were going to be faced with many challenges. If not for the help of godly people who were appalled at the court's orders, it would have been an impossible task. Even the opposing lawyers in the courtroom were stunned and stated that such stern measures were not their intention in opposing the appeal for citizenship, but the courts would not budge.

With our kids leaving Israel and coming home to us in Redding on July 1, we cancelled our trip to Israel in September. We'd been to the Holy Land and had experienced the beauty of being there on previous occasions, and there was no way we were going to leave our road-weary and embattled loved ones for an extended trip anywhere.

Deciding to stay in Redding meant I was still left with the benefit of having my beloved spiritual son, Eddie, back with me in ministry.

When Jason, Alexander, and Tizita returned in September, we were back in full force and ready to rock and roll. We got busy infusing new energy into the ministry, and building upon the foundation of revival Kevin had established. The ministry had always been known for solid teaching and the demonstration of God's love, power, and grace through miracles, signs, and wonders. Our goal was to fan the flames even more and get as many people exposed to His love as possible.

That fall, I led a team of sixteen on a ministry trip to Uganda, and many of the team were from Firestarters. The trip happened two weeks before Thanksgiving. I had to be back for a big family Thanksgiving, so I led the first week and another pastor came in to lead week two.

On this trip, I saw God's power move continuously in ways I'd never seen before. I was the main speaker at a pastor's conference while there and was as nervous as I had ever been in my life! This whole trip was a major step up for me, and to be leading a pastor's conference (called a Leader's Advance) was a tremendous stretch for me. I preached my heart out, but I was positive none of the pastors were relating to a thing I said. All approximately two hundred and fifty leaders sat there stoically with arms folded, seemingly as disconnected from a speaker as an audience can possibly be. When I sat down next to my host, I voiced my consternation, and he said, "Oh no, Pastor Jim, they have been mightily touched. Just wait and see!" He was right. When my team was set to receive the pastors in a prayer line, they came up in droves. It started as a trickle, but once a few brave souls came up, the dam broke and everyone received prayer before they left.

During this ministry time, we witnessed God heal bad backs, twisted arms, and much more, but the most dramatic was those freed from demonic influence. These pastors had all been saved and therefore were possessed by God's Holy Spirit, but many were being influenced and oppressed by curses and spiritual attacks from local witch doctors and other local practitioners of darkness.

We in the West may have a hard time understanding how men and women of God can fall prey to such forces, but believe me, it happens at home, too! It is born from ignorance and believers not understanding the power and authority they carry, authority given to us as the Lord was ascending to heaven. These folks were born and raised around people who believed these dark forces are a lot more formidable than they really are. It's a revelation to them to know that He who lives in them is mightier than he who is in the world.

We saw people thrown to the ground and writhing as they were set free. Others bent in impossible ways, while still others let out inhuman cries and utterings. I proudly saw my team standing strong and praying without fear before I came down to floor level to join them. It was exhausting and invigorating at the same time. We were all so pumped and "high" after that service we really didn't need our buses and vans to take us back to base. We could have floated back. To think I had been so nervous before hand. "Likewise the Spirit also helps in our weaknesses" (Romans 8:26 NKJV).

While on this life-changing ministry trip, our team witnessed events most people have only read about. We didn't count the number of salvations we saw in two weeks, but it had to be several dozen just in the first week, in predominately Muslim villages. One morning, I personally led eleven Muslims to Christ before lunch. As the teams reported back to Show Mercy International, our Ugandan hosts, we heard of whole households and families receiving Jesus as their Lord and Savior.

Some of the areas we were invading were known as "hard" areas to share the gospel, or as areas of "profound darkness" controlled by satanic agents. However, the gospel proved true time and again! Witch doctors would come to a team member, recognizing the true power of Christ, bow down before them, and ask for salvation. Others actually ran away as team members approached these agents of Satan. This was heady stuff, but I was very proud of the team as they stayed grounded in the knowledge it was Christ in them accomplishing all these miracles.

Speaking of miracles, the second week was even wilder than week one. Crusades were held over a three-day period. I turned the team over to my co-leader, Matthew, who arrived on the first day of the week. We debriefed, and I left on day two. Matthew was to lead the crusades that were to take place in the area considered by the locals to be the darkest—the same area we had gone into a few days earlier, only to see the local leaders of darkness flee in terror. The team had prayer-walked this area for an entire day, claiming the entire territory for Christ and inviting the Holy Spirit to come cover the land and its people.

The devil did all he could to stop the Holy Spirit hurricane that was sweeping over this land he had trespassed upon. On the first day of the crusade, an unpredicted rain came and drenched the stage and the people. The sound equipment was sparking and shorting out. It was dangerous. People were soaked, but they remained to hear Matthew deliver the word. From what I was told, he delivered indeed. Matthew had just come from another crusade in another part of the world. Before I left him, he had said he felt power and authority like he had never felt before, and I believe the Holy Spirit had prepared him for a moment such as this. Team members' Facebook postings from Uganda reported that Matthew spoke with awesome power and authority. He stood courageous and strong as the rain poured, the equipment sparked, the speakers actually exploded, and satanic agents taunted him from the crowd that first day.

Then, freedom began to break through. During those three days of the crusade, the team witnessed twice as many salvations as before. People were being healed of skin diseases, lameness, blindness, and deafness. A couple of team members saw snake demons crawling under the skin of a man being set free and exiting his body. Satanic practitioners repented and accepted Jesus as the King of their lives.

A few days before I left, the American and Ugandan missionaries who operate the Show Mercy International base confided in me that though they host teams almost continuously from around the world, they had never seen such kingdom power demonstrated. That, I'm sure, was true—and what they were about to witness in the next few days was going to make the first few days pale in comparison. Every member of our ministry team returned home transformed, including yours truly.

God is so good, and He desperately wants us to partner with Him in setting His people free from oppression. It's not like He needs us. He could do it all on His own, but He wants us involved. If we are going to reign with Christ in heavenly places, then we need to learn to do the stuff now. We are commanded to heal the sick, cleanse the lepers, and raise the dead. He didn't say "if we feel like it" in the original Hebrew—He said we must.

This is our proving ground, our equipping time. A soldier doesn't go into combat with no training; it would be disastrous if he or she did. No, a soldier is trained and equipped to meet the challenge, and so must we be. As His representatives, enlistees in His army, we need to be trained to operate comfortably in the supernatural realms of the kingdom of God. We have our instructions: "And as you go, preach, saying, 'The kingdom of heaven is at hand.' Heal the sick, cleanse the lepers, raise the dead, cast out demons. Freely you have received, freely give" (Matthew 10:7-8 NKJV).

There are times when a believer is granted a revelation that can change his or her life but none more life-changing than the knowledge that Christ lives within us. In Galatians, the apostle Paul says we were nailed to the cross (co-crucified) with Jesus; our old selves no longer exist, but we are now made new. We are a new creation with Christ Jesus living inside of us, in cohabitation with us. Let this sink in. If Christ lives inside us, then there should be no limits to the impact we can have on this fallen world. Jesus said we will do even greater things than He did (see John 14:12). How? Why? Because He is here, in us, beside us, coexisting with us to continue this world's transformation.

The trick is to let Him lead, but most of us have a difficult time doing that. How much are we willing to let Him lead us? Twenty percent? Thirty percent? Perhaps half? If Warren Buffett, a self-made billionaire, came to you and said, "Add my name to all of your financial accounts, including your mortgage and every asset you own, and I'll make you insanely rich! Keep your name on everything as well. You can erase my name from your accounts anytime you'd like. You can even countermand any decisions I make. You can take your financial affairs back over at any time, but I guarantee you that if you let me lead you, I will make you richer than your wildest dreams!" Would you do it? I think most people would not hesitate.

Well, Jesus has given us an even better offer. When He willingly died on that cross, He paid off all of our spiritual debt. The moment we accept Him as our Lord and Savior, He comes to reside inside of us. What a sobering but joy-filled thought: the King lives inside you! What kingdom purpose and mission could you not accomplish in cooperation with Christ?

Jesus became annoyed with the disciples when they feared for their lives during the storm on the lake and woke Him to calm the seas. He wanted so badly for them to understand the authority they could have exercised over the elements themselves, and He wasn't even living inside them yet.

Why walk through life believing you are a pauper when your Dad owns the cattle on a thousand hills? When the Creator of everything is living inside you and wants to manifest life through you? What would life be like if we let Him take control? What glorious riches (not just materially) would we have if we did? What better way to glorify the Creator than to let Him have full reign? Wouldn't it be a glorious adventure to follow Jesus through life just as the disciples had the opportunity to do long ago? It would be, and it is because Christ is living in us right now.

I imagine some people's lives and realities are instantly changed when they grasp this revelation. For most of us, this revelation manifests slowly, over time. For me it has been like peeling through layers of an onion. The more I grasp this, the more I see God's glorious Spirit use me.

Over the next two years, we experienced amazing demonstrations of the Father's love for His children. In Firestarters, we saw tumors thrown up into trash cans, deafness bow to the power of Christ, metal dissolve in bodies, long ugly scars disappear, and much more. On one occasion, a man's leg grew out over five inches. On another, a man crippled with muscular dystrophy was completely healed. He got out of his wheelchair and ran to the other side of campus and back. He also regained his voice, which had been severely impaired. A friend of his, who had continued on in Firestarters class, reported the man gave away his electric wheelchair and went to live on a horse ranch. God healed tinnitus, delivered a woman from severe demonic possession (she had been a Satanist), healed cancer, hundreds of headaches, earaches, and back pain. Nothing is too big or too small for God.

On ministry and missions trips, we've seen blindness and deafness healed, and one man saved from suicide because Joaquin and I got a word of knowledge about him. We told him things about himself we could not have possibly known, which convinced him that God is real. He confessed that before we approached him at the gas station, he was planning to get enough gas to go to a certain spot where he planned to end his life. He left joyful, renewed, and encouraged, knowing he was loved by a good, good Father.

God stretched all of us over the next couple of years. Not only did He demonstrate His awesome sovereignty and love for His people through the signs and wonders listed above, but He continued to put our family in positions and circumstances that both challenged and inspired us all.

Jahi and Kes settled in Spokane, Washington, to help Kes's brother Nehemiah and his wife Shersti with the Gateways Beyond base there. They became Nehemiah's associate leaders there, and Kes led them in awesome worship. The community grew and was active in amazing outreaches in the Spokane area and to nations around the world. Joaquin and Renée continued to minister around the world as itinerant pastors while establishing a ministry called Bethel Activation Ministries (BAM) for other itinerant pastors affiliated with Bethel. Eddie and Maegan were a part of BAM, and Eddie continued to co-lead Firestarters with me while traveling as much as he could with Joaquin.

CHAPTER 24

TEXAS

Joaquin's wife Renée is from Australia. She came to Redding to attend the Bethel School of Supernatural Ministry (BSSM), where she eventually met Joaquin. We are mightily blessed that she did. She traveled the world before coming to Redding to study and learn more about the kingdom, but before coming to the US she had always been attracted to California and Texas—two places she had never been but was drawn to all the same. She had visited some areas of Texas before coming to Bethel to pursue and feed her passion for more of Jesus (she had also served at Hillsong Church in Australia). Renée loved Texas, and fell in love with Austin while visiting the city after her second year of BSSM with her best friend Katie. Even as she and Joaquin were establishing a family and a ministry, God kept speaking to her about Austin.

Joaquin never saw himself as the pastor of a church. He loved travel and the opportunity to meet new people itinerant pastoring brought them, not to mention the satisfaction of seeing God move wherever he went. However, as his family grew, it became increasingly challenging with a wife and two kids (a girl and a boy) to keep up a very demanding itinerant schedule. Either they traveled with the kids or Joaquin would have to leave Renée home alone with two toddlers. Even with Paula and I living right down the street less than a block away, it was still very challenging.

Living in Redding and working at Bethel (by now I was on paid staff) was such an adventure. What a privilege it was to work under the influence of Bill and Beni Johnson, Kris Vallotton and Danny Silk, Eric and Candace Johnson, and Brian and Jenn Johnson. These powerhouses were everyday fixtures for years. It was the home of Jesus Culture, the worship team led by Banning Liebscher, and Bethel Music, the church's worship ministry under Brian and Jenn Johnson. These leaders were changing the world of contemporary Christian music, along with worship coming out of other churches like Hillsong United from Hillsong Church in Sydney, Australia, and other influential Christian groups around the world.

We were at the center of revival. We were where so many wanted to be, but for whatever reason, couldn't be. We were in the eye of the storm, ground zero, a place that was changing how the people of earth related to God and came to realize His kingdom is accessible now. But as is so often the case, Father God had other plans. Like the familiar slogan at the beginning of each *Mission Impossible* movie and TV show, He had an exciting assignment for us, but only "if we choose to accept it!"

For a while, Joaquin had been thinking about making some sort of change. He loved his job and loved serving at Bethel, as we all did, but he was getting restless. God will often create restlessness in us right before asking us to take on something new. My wife and I have experienced a tension in our spirits before God has us move into something or someplace new. I've described it as being like an arrow held tightly by an archer in his drawn bow. An archer cannot hold his bow in a tightly drawn position indefinitely. Soon his muscles begin to quiver as he feels the pressure to release his arrow, before his muscles completely fail, and he can no longer control the bow. It becomes so tense that when God opens the door, points to the target, and says, "Go get 'em," you launch out of the bow with such force you couldn't stop if you tried. It's an exhilarating feeling of total freedom as you fly toward your God-appointed target. Of course, unlike an arrow, we have the freedom to choose. We may be frightened of the unknown. Are there giants waiting to devour us before we reach the goal? Sure! We may also experience feelings of inadequacy, one of the devil's favorite tactics. But we must remember that the devil is a thief and a liar, and he will do his best to convince you that you do not have what it takes to accomplish your ordained mission.

God knows the devil's tactics. But at this point in your life, you've already made your pact with God. He knows you will do what He asks. He just wants you to launch out with as much energy and enthusiasm as possible to keep you hungry and on a victorious trajectory.

After experiencing this tension for a while, one day Joaquin and Renée informed us they were considering planting a church in Austin, Texas. This thought had been percolating in them for quite some time and was now beginning to take shape and form. Joaquin had recently spoken there and was impressed by the unity amongst churches and pastors in Austin, as well as their spiritual hunger. A group of prominent pastors actually spoke to him about coming to Austin to plant a church. They had no idea God had already planted the seed. While flying in on that trip, Joaquin saw a halo over the city from the plane. He took that vision as a positive sign that God had His hand upon Austin. He was encouraged more than ever that he was being called to this region.

While exploring the city, Joaquin and the team discovered a sign that read "Bethel Church Road." At the end of Bethel Church Road was a small church. That was a significant sign of encouragement, but what was even more attention getting was the pair of roadrunner birds they saw running across the street in front of the sign that said, "Bethel Church Road NO OUTLET." Bill Johnson often tells the story about a roadrunner that used to come up to the back window of Bethel Church in Redding during pre-service prayer. Roadrunners are very rare in that part of California. One day, the runner got trapped in the building, got spooked, ran into a glass door, and died. God spoke to Bill and told him that the roadrunner represented the anointing, and if the anointing couldn't get out of the house it would die. Seeing two roadrunners (double portion) on Bethel Church Road, a dead end, signified to Joaquin that the anointing was being "let out of the house and expanding to Austin, Texas!"

God spoke to Joaquin and Renée in several ways over the next few months. Paula and I took a trip to Austin with them and saw firsthand the hunger and enthusiasm amongst some of the area's key spiritual leaders. As momentum grew, Joaquin and Renée began building a team to help partner with them in Austin. The final confirmation that we were following the will of God was when Pastor Bill Johnson blessed the move and gave permission for our church to be an official church plant sent out of Bethel Church Redding. Now, Joaquin and Renée could move forward with the full blessing of the house they were birthed out of.

Eddie and Maegan were already on board when Paula and I decided we would go, as well (prompted by an open vision God gave me of what he was planning for Austin during our first organizing meeting). Now, it was truly a family affair. The small team Joaquin and Renée assembled began to relocate to Austin during the spring and summer of 2017. Eddie and Maegan arrived in August, followed by Joaquin and Renée in September. They began to hold gatherings on a regular basis with those early arrivers in Austin, while the remnant of those still to come met in Redding.

While our group in Redding dwindled as people made the transition to Austin, the Austin group grew rapidly, despite not having a permanent place to meet. Pastors in Austin were very gracious and made space for our people to meet in their churches when available, until the church was able to arrange space in the ballroom of one of the local hotels in South Austin.

As the word spread through the city that Bethel was planting a church, people began to inquire about joining the group. The team set up a series of classes called Elements in a conference room of the hotel designed to expose all those interested to Bethel culture. People wanted to know and experience what living a revival lifestyle meant. This was a brilliant move. Hundreds took the eight-week course that was offered three times from October 2017 through August 2018. Some took the course out of curiosity to see if what they'd heard about Bethel was true. Some took the course and decided it was not for them, and still others who completed the class discovered this was exactly what they'd been looking for and became regular attendees.

Paula and I joined the team in March of 2018 after grooming others to take over our jobs and ministries in Redding. What we saw going on in Austin was amazing. We joined a group of two hundred and fifty to three hundred hungry souls in the ballroom of the Omni Hotel, worshipping God and radically going after more of Him.

Bethel Church Austin officially opened on Saturday, September 21st, 2018. During the inaugural launch conference, over a thousand people joined us to worship God in His goodness and grace. In November 2018, Jahi brought his family to Austin to join us in this magnificent, Holy-Spirit-inspired project.

Fifteen years earlier, God clearly told our family we would all be together in ministry someday. At that time, Jahi had married Kes and was living abroad, part of a Messianic ministry. (They now have four kids: Jacob, Ella, Yeshi, and Josephine.) Eddie was married to Maegan and was working and ministering in the Sacramento area. (They have five girls: Aliah, Alexis, Allie, Ava, and Amoriah.) Joaquin married Renée and was living in Redding while traveling the world spreading God's message through a ministry marked with healing and miracles. Paula and I were living, working, and ministering in Southern California.

When we received that word, we could hardly envision it, but we knew it was true. We could feel it, and the feeling never left any of us. We spoke of it often through the years, all wondering how God was going to make it happen. It seemed unlikely, but we knew God's promises never fail.

Now, here we are in Austin, Texas. Joaquin and Renée are leading the church with three kids now: Kaylah, Asher, and Malaki. They both are amazing teachers. With Joaquin's leadership anointing and Renée's prophetic gifting, they are doing an amazing work for the Lord. Eddie and Maegen are our associate leaders. Eddie preaches often, leads our Men's Ministry, and oversees much more. Maegen directs our children's ministry. Jahi and Kes oversee missions, and several other pastors, and Kes is on our worship team. Paula and I are heading up our Transformation Center (counseling and inner healing ministry), pastoral care, a program called Activate, and our Revival Through Unity program.

Over the years, we have been privileged to witness and participate in mighty moves of God all over the world. We have witnessed revival, mass salvations, mind-boggling healings, deliverances from demonic spirits, and more. But the miracle that makes me love Him all the more is the one unfolding in Austin, Texas. That He would use us to bring His presence, His healing, His revival to a region so desperate for the gospel is truly humbling.

You must allow yourself to dream big. Small dreams don't move mountains, but big dreams lead to big miracles. Maybe you can't sing and dance like Usher or fly through the air like Michael Jordan, but you can do something. God has given us all some sort of talent, some manner of anointing that makes us unique. Find it! If you are anything like me it may take you a while, but trust me, it's there. God did not make carbon copies. Each one of us was created to bring something to the table. We all have a piece of the puzzle, the grand mosaic that is His creation.

Satan will lie to you. He is the father of lies. "When he speaks a lie, he speaks from his own resources, for he is a liar and the father of it" (Mathew 8:44 NKJV). The devil sees your anointing from birth. He is afraid of the potential God has placed in you while you were still in your mother's womb. He will attempt to rob you of your God-given dreams (John 10:10). The devil wants to destroy your future and your destiny. He wants to pervert your talents for his purposes. He will use peer pressure, societal prejudice, and twisted, self-destructive beliefs passed down to you through the generations.

However, I have good news for you. You can rise above all the lies, even above your current circumstances, as I and millions of others have done, by simply accepting Christ as your Lord and believing Jeremiah 29:11, "For I know the thoughts that I think toward you, says the Lord, thoughts of peace and not of evil, to give you a future and a hope" (NKJV). Have faith in yourself and in your Creator. Dream the divine dream and co-create with Him. You may not become President of the United States (or maybe you will), but you can become the president of you as you follow the plan and divine will of the One who created you.

I'm seeing our dreams and God's promises unveiled before my eyes, and it makes my heart swell with love for Him. My sons minister and preach with such power and authority. My wife and daughters lead, sing, preach, teach, and administrate with gifts that could only come from the Father. The apostle Paul wrote in Ephesians 1:3 and 8, "Every spiritual blessing in the heavenly realm has already been lavished upon us as a love gift from our wonderful heavenly Father, the Father of our Lord Jesus—all because he sees us wrapped into Christ.... This superabundant grace is already powerfully working in us, releasing within us all forms of wisdom and practical understanding" (*The Passion Translation*).

In other words, we don't have to earn our Father's love. It is a free gift given to us through the love and sacrifice of our Lord Jesus Christ. I see this superabundant grace working through my wife, sons, daughters-in-love, and grandchildren every day. God has blessed me in my old age to witness His wonderful gifts manifesting in supernatural wisdom, understanding, revelation, and power in them as they serve the kingdom of God and His ordained plan of bringing all of His creation back to Him.

If you have been indecisive about taking the step towards Christ, hesitant to receive Christ as your Lord and Savior, I ask you—what do you have to lose? If all this is a delusion and none of it is real, what does one lose by deciding in favor of accepting it all as truth? More importantly, if all I've shared with you is true—and it is—what do you stand to gain? You stand to gain heaven and eternity with a loving Father and with all your past and current friends and family who have made the right choice together in paradise. Not only will you gain heaven, but as a believer you will begin to experience a miraculous life here on earth as an adopted member and righteous heir in the family of God (Romans 8).

We are all spirit, and we are eternal beings. But the question is, where do you want to spend eternity? Do you want to spend eternity in paradise with a loving Father or eternity in darkness completely shut off from any semblance of love and grace, in torment with eternal regret with no hope of reprieve or escape?

It doesn't matter to God what you have done in the past. That is a part of His grace gift. He holds no account of your past deeds if you wholly accept Him, even in the last hour of your life. It is almost too good to be true, but as amazing as it sounds, it is true. It is a free gift, yours to accept. I pray that you choose the right one.

If you'd like to make the right choice and receive the gift Jesus died to make available to you, go to the Appendix, and you will find a simple prayer you can pray with total sincerity to receive this amazing salvation. As you repeat this prayer of salvation, you will receive the Holy Spirit into your life. I guarantee you will not regret making this choice. Ever!

If you have accepted Jesus as your Lord and Savior, I pray this book has inspired and strengthened you to run your race well with supernatural endurance. I pray that it has emboldened you to share the good news with others and to continue to grow in the Word and in companionship with the Lord. As you grow, find someone to mentor along his or her path as well.

God is truly good and His promises never fail. I stand as His witness that they endure forever!

EPILOGUE

I have three reasons for writing *From the Panthers to the Pulpit*.

First of all, I wanted to leave a written legacy for my grandchildren and great-grandchildren. As long as Paula and I are alive, our story is available and alive in us. Even our sons are old enough to remember the tales being told by friends back in the day when they were still with us. Nonetheless, people fade and memories fade, but the written word, thank God, endures.

My second reason was to bring the hope of Jesus Christ to the hopeless. I was in a deep, dark hole with no apparent way out, but then Jesus. Admittedly, I didn't know it was Him at the time, but trust me it was. It wasn't the devil, because he is a liar. The Word that came to me that day proved to be true and miracle-laden. I was freed from my physical cage, just as that Word said I would. And it was also true that They were not done with me yet. I have been willingly used by God since then to lead many to salvation through His authority and through the demonstration of power through miraculous signs and wonders. If He did it for me, He can and will do it for you.

My third reason in writing this book was to bring a certain perspective to those whose life experience may have been different from mine. My prayer is that readers of this book will say to themselves, "Now I can sort of understand the anger, pain, and frustration that is motivating the events we are witnessing today." With this new perspective, perhaps grace will begin to take root in some hearts. I don't necessarily expect everyone will come into agreement with the tactics used by some, but if we can begin to understand what makes each one of us tick, and how we come to be where we are, then perhaps we can begin to come together to start building bridges across the divide.

Ephesians 2:15 sums it nicely: "Ethnic hatred has been dissolved by the crucifixion of his precious body on the cross. The legal code that stood condemning every one of us has now been repealed by his command. His triune essence has made peace between us by starting over—forming one new race of humanity, Jews and non-Jews fused together!" (*The Passion Translation*).

Unity is not just a good idea, it's God's idea!

I hope my book stirred you to think and to realize that there are possibilities available you may have never thought were there. If you have any questions about this book or about the reality of God, you may reach me at je8tkd@gmail.com. I will try my best to respond in some fashion.

God Bless!

APPENDIX

1) The Holy Spirit

The Holy Spirit is part of the Holy Trinity of the Godhead made up of Father God, Jesus Christ (Son), and the Holy Spirit. The Holy Spirit will come and dwell in those who give their lives to Jesus, proclaim Him as Lord, and recognize that He died and was raised from the dead for the forgiveness of our sins and to reconcile all of us back into proper relationship with Father God. The Spirit will manifest different gifts to those He enters, as He deems appropriate. All of these gifts are magnificent. Some will manifest outwardly and might appear stronger than others, but all are important and equally valuable, just as every part of your body is needed to function properly and one part is no more valuable than the other!

I won't go further in this book, but for more information please find a Spirit-filled church or born-again believer to help you understand this wonderful truth in more detail.

2) A Prayer for Salvation

"Lord, I truly in my heart believe that Jesus Christ is the Son of God and that He died for my sins and for the salvation of my soul. I fully accept Jesus as my Lord and my Savior and I will faithfully and obediently follow Him for the rest of my days. Holy Spirit, I invite you to come into me and I freely receive you and all Your gifts. Amen!"

If you sincerely prayed this prayer, then you are born again and have been adopted into God's family with all the rights, privileges, and authority reserved for a son or daughter of the Most High King!

3) Revival: An Awakening in a Church or Community

An outpouring of the SPIRIT OF GOD on His people!

> "And it shall come to pass afterward
> That I will pour out My Spirit on all flesh;
> Your sons and your daughters shall prophesy,
> Your old men shall dream dreams,
> Your young men shall see visions.
> And also on My menservants and on My maidservants
> I will pour out My Spirit in those days."
> (Joel 2:28-29 NKJV)

4) More on Korea

Master KI-Whang Kim was the savior of Korea, as were many like him. After the Korean War, Korea was left in a complete state of devastation. South Korea suffered close to one million casualties. The war claimed an estimated total of 2.5 million casualties for all those involved. The war between North and South Korea officially began in June of 1950, though there had been frequent fighting between the two sides, fortified by their allies, since WWII.

During its course, the war waged back and forth over the 38th parallel for years, and Seoul changed hands four times during the first year of fighting alone. The initial North Korean attack pushed the unprepared South Korean army back into a very small tip of the country until UN forces responded. The response from the Allies pushed the disorganized North Korean troops back into their territory all the way to the Amnok (Yalu) River (the border between North Korea and China), which prompted China's involvement![3]

Both countries were devastated, and when the conflict ended in 1953, half of all industry in South Korea had been destroyed along with a third of all homes! Social and political disorder was the rule of the day, and thousands of widows and orphans in the hundreds-of-thousands were left to be cared for. Unemployment was rampant, and corruption was widespread under the reign of President Syngman Rhee. The Republic of South Korea received millions of dollars in aid from a multitude of friendly nations, but between the corruption of the government and the inexperience of political leaders to govern, this aid was far from enough.[4]

In time, the country began to establish a fledgling export industry, and in a brilliant and innovative move they decided to export one of the country's most valuable assets: martial arts! Koreans developed many different types of fighting arts over the centuries: soft styles, hard styles, throwing styles, striking styles, and so forth, as had most Asian cultures. The country had been heavily influenced by the fighting styles of China and Japan while occupied at different times in its history by both these nations. Now, combining its own original styles with the best of the fighting styles of these two cultures, it had developed a form that was one of the most devastating, complete, and effective in the history of the world! American GIs from both the conflicts in Korea and Vietnam came home raving about the Korean fighting methodologies.

A few short years after the war's end, the Korean government decided to "export" some of its most accomplished taekwondo masters to the richest nations of the world. Taekwondo was a marriage of a majority of the Korean martial art kwans (organizations) such as: Moo Duk Kwan, Sang Do Kwan, Chang Do Kwan, Ji Do Kwan, Chi Do Kwan, and a few others brought together under one unified umbrella. Master Kim had been one of the major architects of this unification. The idea was to propagate taekwondo throughout the world, and a percentage of the monies generated from dues, membership fees, and equipment sales were then sent back to Korea to help in the recovery of this small, devastated, war-torn nation. Millions of people worldwide, including myself, have been the beneficiaries of this farsighted strategy.

Taekwondo is now taught and practiced in practically every nation in the world. It is an Olympic sport and has over two hundred nations participating in the Olympics and other international, regional, national, and local competitions. It generates hundreds of millions of dollars annually. Right from its very beginning, this plan proved to be fruitful and beneficial both financially and psychologically to a nation desperately needing a boost to its wallet and its national pride.

My first experience with taekwondo began the day I started lessons from Master Kim at the YMCA, but it has continued until today, over fifty years later, and that man's influence still resonates in my life today. The basic tenants of taekwondo are courtesy, integrity, perseverance, self-control, and indomitable spirit. These standards to live by have sustained me through many trials and challenges (especially before I made God an integral part of my life), and they continue to do so today. Honor and respect are paramount in the martial arts and every student, from beginner to advanced status, is taught to live by these credos from the very beginning if the art is taught properly.

Master Kim established a class in the heart of DC and took a bunch of young men with distraction-filled lives and doubtful futures and introduced an attitude into their psyches of "never say die" and "never quit" no matter the circumstances. He taught us we could achieve a great deal more than we realized in life with the right attitude and an indomitable spirit. The right attitude could take us a long way in life. He personally taught me, first, I could take a lot (physically and emotionally) without breaking, and second, size doesn't matter when you have heart.

REFERENCES

[1] *God's Generals: Why They Succeeded and Why Some Failed,* by Roberts Liardon, 1999. Published by Whitaker House in the USA.

[2] *Azusa Street: They Told Me Their Stories*; the Youth and Children of Azusa Street Tell Their Stories, by Tom Welchel, 2006. Published by McCowan and Morris Publishing Company, Printed in the USA.

[3] Korean War Casualties and Statistics: *HistoryGuy.com*

[4] Korean Enigma page: *www.cotf.edu*

Made in the USA
Monee, IL
05 January 2022